INSIGHTS

CONVERSATIONS WITH

Theodor Reik

Books by Theodor Reik

Freud as a Critic of Culture
   (*in German*)
How One Becomes a Psychoanalyst
   (*in German*)
Ritual (*With a preface by*
   Sigmund Freud)
The Unknown Murderer
Surprise and the Psychoanalyst
From Thirty Years with Freud
Masochism in Modern Man
A Psychologist Looks at Love
Psychology of Sex Relations
Dogma and Compulsion
Listening with the Third Ear
Fragment of a Great Confession
The Secret Self
The Haunting Melody
The Search Within
Creation of Woman
Mystery on the Mountain
The Temptation
Myth and Guilt
Of Love and Lust
The Compulsion to Confess
Sex in Man and Woman
Jewish Wit
The Need to Be Loved
Pagan Rites in Judaism
Voices from the Inaudible
Curiosities of the Self
The Many Faces of Sex

INSIGHTS

CONVERSATIONS WITH
Theodor Reik

BY ERIKA FREEMAN

PRENTICE-HALL, INC.

Englewood Cliffs, New Jersey

Insights: Conversations with Theodor Reik

by Erika Freeman

Copyright © 1971 by Erika Padan Freeman and
The Estate of Theodor Reik

ISBN—0-13-467563-0
Library of Congress Catalog Card Number: 77-155768

Printed in the United States of America   T

Prentice-Hall International, Inc., London
Prentice-Hall of Australia, Pty. Ltd., Sydney
Prentice-Hall of Canada, Ltd., Toronto
Prentice-Hall of India Private Ltd., New Delhi
Prentice-Hall of Japan, Inc., Tokyo

*To my father Arthur Gross,
to my father surrogate Theodor Reik,
to my husband Paul,
and to all men who reason through love
and love through reason*

CONTENTS

INTRODUCTION

Theodor Reik was a protégé, student, and lifelong friend of Sigmund Freud. He was also a member of the pioneering circle of psychoanalysts that was headed by Freud and included Carl Jung, Alfred Adler, Otto Rank, Hans Sachs, Sandor Ferenczi—men whose very names are synonymous with psychoanalysis. Of those in that early circle, Reik became Freud's favorite and the man Freud thought of as his *Nachfolger*—successor. Freud had been disappointed and hurt by what he considered defections by Jung, Adler, and Rank. But Reik never broke with Freud. He never entered into competition with him. Instead he enlarged upon and deepened the areas that Freud had explored. Perhaps he did so because Freud had become his father surrogate—for when they met, Reik was twenty-two and had lost both his parents, and Freud was fifty-four.

While a student at the University of Vienna, Reik had begun exploring the revolutionary science of psychoanalysis, and when it came time for him to write his doc-

toral dissertation he chose to do a psychoanalytic study of
Flaubert's *The Temptation of St. Anthony*. This was the
first such interpretation of a literary work ever written,*
and when it was completed Reik sent it to Freud who,
impressed with what he read, asked Theodor Reik to call
upon him. Thus began a lasting relationship.

Freud convinced Reik not to go to medical school
in order that he could be trained in psychoanalysis
that much sooner. He then arranged for Karl Abraham to
analyze Reik, and for several years Freud helped to support Reik financially. As a result, Theodor Reik became
one of the first non-medical psychoanalysts and the first
whom Freud had personally dissuaded from becoming a
physician. Freud, of course, was embroiled for many years
in the controversy over non-medical practitioners of psychoanalysis. It was particularly in defense of Theodor Reik,
however, that he wrote *The Question of Lay Analysis*, as
someone had decided to make a test case by suing Dr.
Reik for malpractice, or "quackery," or some such
nonsense because Reik was a doctor but not a physician.
The Question of Lay Analysis proved to be a defense well
taken, since, in addition to the hypocrisy it implicitly laid
bare, Theodor Reik went on to become one of the titans
of psychoanalysis. Freud's arguments were prophetic, too,
for of the major contributions to psychoanalysis since his
death, surely some of the most significant have been made
by non-medical analysts, Erich Fromm and Erik Erikson
among them.

Perhaps it should be pointed out that the term "lay
analysis" has been replaced with "non-medical analysis."
When Freud used "lay analysis" in the title of his work,
he was deliberately calling upon the concept then current.
He began the book's introduction, however, by equating

* 1911-1912

"lay" with "non-medical" and went on to state, "It may prove to be the case that in this instance the patients are not like other patients, laymen are not, properly speaking, laymen, and physicians not precisely what one is entitled to expect in this connection and what should entitle them to the claim to be the sole practitioners." *

In 1938 the threat of Nazi take-over caused Dr. Reik to leave the Netherlands, where he was in private practice and lecturing at the university in Leiden. When he arrived in New York he found that American psychoanalysts still adhered to the dictum that psychoanalysts who were not also physicians were not entitled to practice psychoanalysis. Thus for some time no patients were referred to Dr. Reik, and therefore he had no opportunity to practice his art (for as he practiced it, psychoanalysis is an art), nor to help those whom he could have helped. As a result his source of livelihood was cut off. But perhaps, as he later felt, it was for the best, because he had to turn to his talent for writing.

Among his first works was the now classic and indispensable—certainly to analysts—*Listening with the Third Ear.* That book introduced a new phrase into the American vernacular and catapulted Theodor Reik into public prominence. In addition, Reik founded the National Psychological Association for Psychoanalysis, a training center for non-medical analysts.

By now the battle concerning non-medical psychoanalysis is essentially over and is only being nursed along by a few diminishing pockets of resistance within the medical profession who feel it necessary to cling to the old system. Indeed, except for those bastions of organizationally-ossified attitudes, the question has largely become academic, especially since the great among the medical

* Sigmund Freud, *The Question of Lay Analysis,* tr. by Nancy Procter-Gregg, (New York: W. W. Norton & Co., 1950), p. 15.

psychoanalysts, men such as Kurt Eissler,* Lawrence Kubie, Gustav Bychowski, Karl Menninger, and others, have long since left that parochialism behind.

The first long talk that Dr. Reik and I had was a rather spirited one, and he invited me to visit him and continue our conversation. When I arrived at his office he was wearing a pale gray doctor's coat, and, as always, he was smoking. As I looked around the room, he pointed to the wall behind his desk, which was covered with pictures of Freud, and he said, "You see all those pictures of Freud? There are fifty of them. Some are from the Congresses, some from The Hague, and so on. He was my friend and teacher, and he was like a father to me."

The character of the men who create a new movement influences to a great degree the direction of that movement; and the kind of people they are, the quality of humanity they demonstrate, determines to a great extent the kind of people who are drawn to the movement. But as the originators die, succeeding generations frequently become pale copies of them or imitations of what they imagine their predecessors were. They often ossify their predecessors into static, uncreative positions, turning their concepts into fixed laws instead of using their attitudes as examples that provide direction. To follow in the spirit of a pathfinder does him more honor than merely to follow in his footsteps. And if that spirit moves one to take a new step, than that step should be taken.

Reik followed in the spirit of Freud, but as his own work as psychoanalyst, teacher, and writer testifies, he did not fear taking new steps. It was, then, to further illustrate the quality of the man, his attitudes and how he related to others, that this book came into being. I wanted to share the experience of being with him, of be-

* See Eissler, K. R., *Medical Orthodoxy and the Future of Psychoanalysis* (N. Y.: International Universities Press, 1965).

coming acquainted with his thought processes, with how he felt about matters large and small, even with how he sounded; to convey a sense of who Dr. Reik was as a human being, as a man who understood human weaknesses, his own as well as those of others; a man who did not judge, to whom nothing that was human was alien. In short, I wanted others to experience on a personal level one of the founding fathers of psychoanalysis. For the quality of a person, the texture and substance, shapes the way in which he practices his profession, and with a man such as Reik, the very profession itself.

Theodor Reik was a simple man in a complicated way, as all simple and true matters are complicated. He was so un-assuming and his insights were so attuned to the heart of situations that he made much of what he said seem self-evident. In fact, those who recognized only the jargon-laden phrase or were accustomed to listening only at the level of cliché often missed the significance of what he said. Reik himself never used jargon, yet he was tolerant of those of us still young enough to be using it. But if one was with him long enough, somehow the jargon be-came superfluous. It was no longer necessary to use it to prove that one was a *bona fide* member of the fraternity.

We have all been filled with catch-phrases and obscur-ities, and we have been subjected to any number of books designed more to demonstrate the erudition of the writer than to teach us. As Freud had been, so Reik was concerned with teaching and with understanding and with being understood. Above all, to understand and to be understood. He wanted to help us comprehend a seemingly lawless ter-ritory with its own irrevocable laws and principles; to take us beneath the surface of our assumptions and of that which we take for granted so that we may learn the nature of that two-thirds of the iceberg that lies submerged; to help us become navigators on the primal sea in all of us, the unconscious. It is not enough to see with the eye or to understand only that which we can cause to be mechanically reproduced, because, while real and valuable and necessary, these processes do not reveal the whole truth. We must also learn to sail by sonar.

One wishes that all things were logical, yet as they are, they have their own logic. Some are, if you will, psychologic, and the laws that describe them are different in kind, even as the laws of geometry in outer space are different from the geometry of Pythagoras—whereas on earth the shortest distance between two points is a straight line, in space the shortest distance between two points is a curve. Theodor Reik was among the first to try to fathom this other logic, this other private life we all have that controls, whether we will it or not, the public life we lead.

Yet one of Reik's most endearing characteristics was that he never took himself too seriously. One day I brought him a chapter I had arranged for this book, and after reading it he commented, "You must not make me sound so formal, not even in print. If I am funny, then laugh at me." The next version I brought made him laugh heartily. Then he said, "But they will not understand what we are laughing about—and that to laugh is serious."

He spoke simply, and while discussing one subject, ranged over many in a sort of continuing free association. I am told that not everyone was enamored of these verbal excursions. For myself, I found them delightful and, perhaps because I, too, am discursive in that way, I did not always realize that we were on such an excursion. Indeed, at first I had hoped to reproduce the conversations exactly as they had been, just to illustrate the adventure and humor of his free associations. But it was pointed out that in a book of this sort one should follow the general thought sequence to which people are accustomed. Some of the conversations, therefore, were rearranged in order to group them into approximate chapters, but I did try to retain the quality of his spontaneity and discursiveness.

Many of the subjects we covered have been discussed more fully and scholarly in Dr. Reik's own books, yet there are things said in conversation that illumine well-scholared areas, for as we read a book we frequently do not make the same assumptions the author does as he writes. And so sometimes I played the devil's advocate or asked what we used to call *Klotz-kashes*, elementary questions, to see what his response would be. Dr. Reik always directed himself to the question, but with that twinkle in his eye with which he indicated that he knew what I was up to. We also discussed some of the "rules" that are assumed to govern the attitudes and behavior of psychoanalysts, as these have given rise to stereotyped notions of what analysts say, think, or do. For example, on the whole it is considered undesirable for an analyst to accept gifts from his patients. But what was Freud's attitude about it? And there is the question of "fractured analysis," about which very little is known or written. Or the fact that Freud used to complain about what he called "the Sunday crust"—which is to say, the effect of the one day, Sunday, when the patient did not see his psychoanalyst.

Dr. Reik and I talked, too, about some of the everyday matters that arise in psychoanalysis and that, in accordance with the way they are dealt with, may eventually contribute to a technique or a theory in the psychoanalytic scheme of things. We did not necessarily discuss things that are "relevant" by today's definitions. It is the analyst's contention that everything is relevant to the human experience; he cannot be bound by the dicta of those who insist that current and immediate problems are all one has a right to involve himself with. That way lies tyranny of thought, no matter how well-intentioned the concern.

For many years, Dr. Reik came to our house for Sunday

brunch, and he would tease me and say that the only reason he came was that I made good scrambled eggs. But those brunches took on a special significance. On the first day of his vacation a few years ago he fell and broke his hip. When I visited him in the hospital, he told me the dream he had had the night before. The dream indicated so clearly a real wish to die that I became frightened and did the only thing I could. I yelled at him: "How dare you die now. We've been working together, and because of that I have a lot of enemies. But I'm not ready to face them yet. I could have made my way by myself in my own good time, but now it's different. And you want to just go off and leave me, my reputation only half earned, enemies not yet deserved. How could you do such a thing, especially after you said you considered me your *Nachfolger?*" He looked surprised and the twinkle crept back into his eyes, so I continued, more calmly now: "And besides, if you get well, I'll come to your house and make the eggs." He smiled and said weakly, "No, I'll come to your house."

During our brunches we discussed mundane matters, as well as serious concerns. Referring to this book, which I was slow in finishing, he would say, "Erika I will build you a monument to procrastination"; but always with a smile. We usually invited a few other friends, too, and Dr. Reik would tell stories or test out a theory he had. Once he presented a theory with which one of our friends disagreed tellingly. "Well," Dr. Reik answered, "then it is not a good theory."

Reik seemed to be the compleat psychoanalyst. He felt the part, he looked the part, he even spoke the part. In his courtly way he told me, "You wear our mantle well, so to speak. You are Viennese, you are Jewish, you are a refugee, you think the same way we did, but you are prettier. On the other hand, you have lost perhaps too much of your accent, hm? Do you realize that the thicker the accent, the more you could charge? At least that is what one of my students told me."

Reik was a gentle and modest man. Above all, he loved and revered Freud, and he never esteemed his own gifts as much as he valued his relationship with Freud. In fact, he tended to be self-deprecating, too much so for his own good, and that was something about which Freud had chided him a good deal. Eventually Reik himself gave it a name, He called it *social masochism*, as differentiated from *sexual masochism*, and it is a term that has been absorbed into much of the psychoanalytic literature. Because of my association with him, I have come to think that social masochism in a reasonable dose, that is to say as a dynamic rather than a pathology, may be a necessary component of the character structure of the psychoanalyst, if only because he must be able to take abuse from his patients in the transference without becoming defensive or punitive.

Remarkable enough in any age, Reik was even more extraordinary in ours, for he was a genuine humanist, dedicated to the fulfillment of the individual. To him, everybody was somebody. He always listened attentively to whomever he was with, as though it were generally understood that everyone had something valuable to say. One felt more intelligent when he listened. Even as he grew older, Reik retained a close association with everyday life, and much of his wisdom was drawn from everyday experiences. Nothing was too mundane for his interest and concern, for his observation and interpretation. He was always full of wonderment. Nor was anything too "special" or out of the ordinary for his further study. When we first began to work together, he insisted that he was an old man and that he would not write anymore. About six months later he said, "Let's work together on a book about the repetition

compulsion of the Jews." But we did not agree in that area
as we did not agree in others. Since that time, however, he
produced three books of his own, the last of which, *The
Many Faces of Sex*, I think of as a kind of psychoanalytic-
Zen.

That he was never titanized was partly in the nature of
Reik's personality. He was good, and gentle, and simple.
That makes for great humanity. But he was not rude
enough for lionization. For that, one must be more self-
aggrandizing and care less for other people's feelings. He
was, if one can say such a thing about a great man, truly
sweet. He was so unassuming that it did not strike one
at first how remarkable that was for a man in his position.
In a world of self-glorification he was genuinely modest.

His work was revolutionary. Because of it we understand
better the dynamics of guilt, of masochism, of compulsion;
of the psychology of ritual, of religion, of literature and
music; the nature of love. His study of the psychology of
women began long before it became fashionable, and although in some of our conversations he sounded like a
gentleman of the old school, his understanding of women
was acute and profound. Above all, we are indebted to him
for the insight he gave us into the processes of the analytic
mind at work. His *Listening With the Third Ear* is, in fact,
the most important example we have of what Freud called
"free-floating attention." Reik demonstrated great courage
in exposing to us his own free associations to illustrate the
private and necessarily convoluted routes which the analyst's mind must take to reach an understanding of his
patient's unconscious.

On the base of a statue at the University of Vienna is in-
scribed: *Nur ein guter Mensch kann ein guter Arzt sein.*
"Only a good human being can be a good doctor." Theodor Reik was both.

Erika Padan Freeman

INSIGHTS
CONVERSATIONS WITH
Theodor Reik

PSYCHOANALYSIS

Dr. Freeman: How would you define psychoanalysis?

Dr. Reik: I would define psychoanalysis first as a method of finding unconscious, repressed, and disavowed contents, and then as a method of treating neurotic and borderline cases of psychosis.

Dr. Freeman: Would you say that psychoanalysis is appropriate for everybody?

Dr. Reik: No, certainly not. There are certain indications for deciding when analysis could be applied and when it could not be.

Dr. Freeman: What indications, for instance, would signify one should apply psychoanalysis?

Dr. Reik: For a full developed psychosis, I would say psychoanalysis is not applicable.

Dr. Freeman: But neuroses would be amenable?

Dr. Reik: Neurosis, yes.

Dr. Freeman: How can one judge whether or not a patient's analysis has been successful?

DR. REIK: By two criteria. First, whether the patient is now able to work without perfectionism symptoms and anxieties. And second, whether the patient is able to love another person without the influx of too great a hostility towards that person. Those should be the two major aims to be reached.

We have to remove inhibitions from the patient's life. But we have no right to fashion the patient after our image, because we are not God. He should only have to fulfill his own potentialities, which could be quite different from ours.

DR. FREEMAN: What if a patient can work but only with a great deal of anxiety?

DR. REIK: Then our aim is not reached.

DR. FREEMAN: But if you have a patient who doesn't work well, and when he does work he is always anxious —yet there seems to be no reason; there seems to be no profound disturbance . . .

DR. REIK: No, anxiety is a profound disturbance. Of course you have a great many cases in which psychoanalysis can only improve a certain condition—and even cases in which we can consider it a success to maintain the patients at a certain level. In Ferenczi's book, *Theory of Neurosis,* there is a diagnosis of a case that states: "Case of schizophrenia by means of psychoanalysis kept on the level of an obsessional neurosis through many years." So in that sense analysis helped.

DR. FREEMAN: So things that cannot be cured must be endured.

DR. REIK: Yes. You can only play with the cards in your hand. Sometimes a patient has destroyed his life to such an extent that you only do the best for him that you can.

DR. FREEMAN: He went out to build a palace and there are just enough bricks left to build a little cottage. So we should help him build the cottage.

In other words we have to differentiate between what is a characteristic trait and what is a neurotic trait.

DR. REIK: That's right.

I think in general we have a very favorable chance for a successful analysis with a man when we see that he is ambitious. A man should be ambitious. If he is not ambitious then our chance is less good. Just as a woman should be vain. If she is not vain then we have no chance. Sometimes in supervision, I see a woman who goes out and does not look into a mirror. I get doubtful about her. I would imagine that a woman who passes a mirror should look into it. Except when she is in a terrible hurry or her child is in danger.

DR. FREEMAN: I have a patient who won't look in a mirror. She knows she is vain but she is terribly ashamed of it. At home that was one of the worst things you could be—a vain girl.

DR. REIK: No, that is neurotic. Generally, I would say that when a woman has a chance to look into the mirror and she doesn't do it, unless there are strong reasons, I get suspicious that she is not very feminine.

DR. FREEMAN: What if she has some doubts about her looks? Every time she looks at herself she thinks she is ugly?

DR. REIK: Oh, no, no. I was in the elevator and there was a young woman. An older woman came into the elevator and talked with her and she said: "You know I couldn't stand to look at myself. So I went to the hairdresser then to the manicurist and then I bought a new dress." That is their salvation.

DR. FREEMAN: And if she is hopeless about her looks?

DR. REIK: There is no such thing. I don't believe it. And I don't believe it because I have two daughters, and I know how they work. Let's say we are sitting in a restaurant and a woman comes in and each of my daughters looks her over, but good, believe me. And then each of them knows whether she bought her dress at an expensive shop or a cheap one. But a woman works with the compensation mechanism. She says to herself: "That woman has wonderful blonde hair, but I have beautiful eyes." My daughter told me that. I would say that this is feminine, to work with the compensation mechanism. So that is good, because you cannot have everything.

DR. FREEMAN: Many people who consider going into analysis worry about the cost. Do you think financial difficulty is a valid reason for avoiding psychoanalysis?

DR. REIK: There must be some hardship or it can't work.

DR. FREEMAN: Can you give us an example of a successful analysis?

DR. REIK: For instance, I could tell you a case I saw the other day, when a woman had a sudden block in writing. She was a college professor and had published a few books; but now she had a sudden writing block, which was unexplained. The situation was the following: Her mother, who had a weak heart, got very seriously ill and had to have an operation. The daughter waited at the hospital and was prepared that at any moment a doctor or a nurse would come to tell her that her mother had died on the operating table. To her astonishment, mother survived and made a quick recovery.

And now, the daughter suddenly could not write a book which had a certain deadline. She could not write it at all. Then she came to me and thought I could free her from this block in a short time. I didn't succeed in a short time, but I succeeded, to a certain extent, in a longer time. The explanation of this block was the following: It seems she expected her mother to die and she was waiting, unconsciously, until mother dies, after which time she was prepared to continue with her book and finish it.

DR. FREEMAN: And her mother's staying alive deprived her of this opportunity?

DR. REIK: Yes, her mother still lives, but nevertheless, eventually she overcame that and she has written the book now.

DR. FREEMAN: And you explained this to her?

DR. REIK: Yes.

DR. FREEMAN: And she accepted it?

DR. REIK: Yes, she accepted it finally—after some resistance.

DR. FREEMAN: Would you say that analysis is also appropriate for children?

DR. REIK: Oh, yes. I can give you an example which is quite near in character to the one I just mentioned. There was a little girl of 9, who didn't want to go to school. She said she would go to school only on one condition— that mother was in the same classroom or in the room nearby. The school psychologist gave a deadline and said that if the girl doesn't come to school by a certain time he will send her to a school for retarded children, although she was quite intelligent. The deadline forced us to realize —a student of mine, who was under my supervision then—that we would have to explain to this little girl that the fact that she wants her mother to be in the same room or in the neighboring room is caused by the thought that mother would die if the little girl doesn't see her or isn't certain that mother's nearby. Behind this thought was certainly an unconscious death wish against mother.

DR. FREEMAN: Did the analyst tell this to the child?

DR. REIK: Yes, she did—it was a woman analyst. She told her after a short time. At first the little girl rejected that information. But then the girl accepted it and had great success.

DR. FREEMAN: What does this illustrate as a requirement for what the analyst must understand?

DR. REIK: The analyst must understand the point of gravity. The decisive point for the patient is not just in the understanding any more but in the re-experiencing, even living through these emotions again, and overcoming them, conquering them, mastering them.

DR. FREEMAN: And forgiving yourself for having had them?

DR. REIK: Yes, and forgiving yourself for having had them, and understanding that it's human to have them.

DR. FREEMAN: But it doesn't stop there, does it?

DR. REIK: No, it doesn't. It goes on further to other symptoms and other fears. There is never only one single symptom, of course. There is always a collection.

DR. FREEMAN: How would you describe your technique as differing from Freud's, if it differs at all?

DR. REIK: Yes, I would say that it differs in certain directions. We have made some modification in the technique of Freud which is conditioned by the fact that, for instance, sexual knowledge is pervasive now, while, in the time of Freud, you could not mention sex at first, or only with great caution. It's now allowed to discuss it, even in the first interview. Freud told us once—don't forget he lived in the Victorian Age—that when he was a young resident in Vienna, a mother came with her 19-year-old daughter who had some throat troubles. Freud wanted to examine her and the daughter said, full of indignation: "I don't let such a young doctor to look into my throat!" At the time, of course, that kind of reaction was possible. It would not be possible today.

DR. FREEMAN: When people come into analysis, they very often ask for some basic rules.

DR. REIK: Yes, there is a basic rule. Namely, you should say everything which occurs to you. Freud turned my attention to these lines from Kipling's poem *If*, which you should know. They illustrate free-association: "If you can think and not make thoughts your aim." And in analysis you should say everything as you would ordinarily say it. I'll give an instance of that. I treated once a sailor in Asheville, North Carolina, where I was a consulting psychologist during vacation. He was being treated by a lady psychiatrist who didn't make much progress with him and who asked me to have an interview with him. So I talked with him. He had been dismissed from the Navy on account of his depression. So I asked him directly about his sex life. And he said: "Well, I said to the doctor that whenever I have intimate union with a girl, that and that happens." I said: "I never heard an American sailor call that 'intimate union.'" To which he said: "But the doctor is a lady." Of course, it meant something, in the South especially. So I asked his lady doctor to transfer this patient to a male physician.

Also, at some point in the analysis you have to make sure the patient understands what is meant by "unconscious," "repressed," and so on. I remember once Freud gave a lecture in the Psychiatric Institute where the audience was mixed, physicians and laymen. He spoke about repression. He used the following comparison: "Let us assume that in this audience, which follows me with such wonderful attention, there is a man who makes noises that disturb us. You try to quiet him down. He refuses. Finally two of you throw him out of the door." Freud was saying that this is what happens in repression: Something that is too disturbing to accept is pushed out of consciousness. Then Freud described the return of the repressed material: "But this man who is outside the door doesn't keep quiet. He shouts that he wants to come back and make trouble. Someone goes to the door and says, 'Look here, my dear fellow, when you promise to keep quiet we'll let you in.' " That is what we do in analysis. We let the repressed in so it won't do anymore disturbing.

DR. FREEMAN: You mentioned asking that the sailor be sent to a male analyst, but do you find that there is some prejudice against women analysts or European analysts by American patients?

DR. REIK: Perhaps only those that lose, so to speak the character of a personal experience in analysis which Freud always emphasized. It should be a personal experience. That does not mean that you are sharing all the inner experiences of the patient. It means only that you have to, so to speak, have a taste of it. When a housewife wants to find out how her soup tastes, she will not eat a full plateful of soup, she will take a little spoon and taste the soup.

DR. FREEMAN: But ordinarily, you wouldn't say that it matters very much whether a patient went to a male or female analyst?

DR. REIK: In general, not.

DR. FREEMAN: But are there some particular indications when they should.

DR. REIK: There are particular indications, for instance, homosexuality, or a conflict with mother, or the early death of mother, there are such. I once treated a man who could only have sexual intercourse with Aryan girls, and especially Nazi girls. No one who resembled his mother or sisters.

DR. FREEMAN: And those would indicate female analysts?

DR. REIK: Female analysts, yes.

DR. FREEMAN: And does the same thing hold true for . . .

DR. REIK: For men.

DR. FREEMAN: In other words, a female homosexual would then go to a male analyst? But those would be the only indications where it would matter?

DR. REIK: Yes. But even there not always.

DR. FREEMAN: Someone I heard about said he would only want a woman analyst and she had to be very beautiful.

DR. REIK: That may be because he is an aesthete, a visual type.

DR. FREEMAN: I had the impression that "visual type" was just an excuse. Eventually, because of his hostility towards women, he went to a man, because, by definition, all women are terrible.

DR. REIK: That happens also.

DR. FREEMAN: Many people feel that psychoanalysts are concerned primarily with sexual matters and that the basis of everybody's problem is sexual.

DR. REIK: That's not correct. It's only correct in so far as the sexual behavior of the person is, so to speak, pattern-forming for the behavior in other, not sexual, directions. But sexuality, in its gross meaning at least, has by no means the importance which the layman gives it when he speaks about analysis, analytic theory.

DR. FREEMAN: Could you explain what an analyst means by sexuality?

DR. REIK: In Freud's original theory, it included sympathy, tenderness, affection and so on, our sublimated expressions of sexuality. For instance, the feeling towards a friend; the feeling towards the parent of the same sex, and so on.

DR. FREEMAN: Do you think that we've gotten too specific in the way we deal with sexuality now? That when people speak of this, they speak of it as a specifically directed area rather than what was meant originally by sexuality, namely the sense of life—that relationship which deals with others in any kind of feeling, and not necessarily an area which belongs to so-called morals?

✻

DR. FREEMAN: If a so-called normal person comes into one's office and says, "I don't feel very well. I feel very sad. . . ."

DR. REIK: So we'd find out why he feels sad. Why he's depressed. That would take considerable time, of course, if it's only emotional—as vague as you say.

DR. FREEMAN: But would you say that the ordinary feelings of depression and elation, within a certain range, tend to be normal—everyone would have them?

DR. REIK: Yes, from time to time.

DR. FREEMAN: At what stage then would we think that they were more than normal?

DR. REIK: It's pathological when it relates very deep and lasts a long time. What is depression? Depression is rage against someone else turned inside against yourself. When the analyst succeeds in bringing the patient to an outbreak of rage, then the patient is over the hump so to speak—he doesn't feel so depressed and the depression soon will disappear.

Freud once showed me a little cartoon. In this cartoon you see a man who is sitting at his desk and there is a photograph of a woman before him. It seems the woman has deserted him or thrown him over or was unfaithful, and he has a pistol in his hand. And he raises the pistol and wants to kill himself. Then he lowers the pistol and shoots the photograph, which is very good. It means that the aggression is first turned inside and then the aggression is turned outside, symbolically. He doesn't kill the woman —he kills the picture. That is as in analysis—he talks about it, without carrying out murderous wishes and rages, without acting them out, so to speak.

DR. FREEMAN: Then suicide, for instance, would that be partly . . .

DR. REIK: Suicide would follow the same mechanisms as depression. But if a person who is in analysis attempts suicide, or even succeeds, then his knowledge about himself was only intellectually accepted. It has true effect only if it is also emotionally accepted. There are, of course, certain other cases, but in general, it is thought that suicide is based on a death wish against a person who is near and dear to the patient. Let me make the difference clear. When you walk on Broadway, let's say, and there is a man who steps on your toe and you have a corn there, it hurts terribly, so you have only one thought, namely, "Drop dead!" And it doesn't bother you. But when such a thought would come up against your father, your mother, your child, it would percolate and would have emotional consequences and would lead to certain emotional conflicts.

DR. FREEMAN: Which will be unacceptable.

DR. REIK: Because the premise is different in that case. About a stranger you don't give a damn, but about your father and mother you care for them. I give you a personal instance of that. My first wife, Ella was her name, died of a heart disease after many years of illness.

DR. FREEMAN: How old was she?

DR. REIK: When she died she was 48. But it was a terrific strain on me financially all those years, because she had to go very often for a cure to a sanatorium. She had kidney trouble besides that. And every time she went, I spent long hours with her in the sanatorium in Vienna and later in Berlin. And Freud once told me I shouldn't do that. I should go there for ten, fifteen minutes, and go

away, and then return the next day for ten, fifteen minutes. And he said that on account of the following: Very
often when I used to leave the sanatorium I got dizzy
spells. Once when I got dizzy I fell down, so I had to be
brought by ambulance back home. It was so bad that the
doctors at first thought it is nicotine poisoning, then
they thought it is Ménière's disease, the middle ear disease.
But Freud said it must be that I identify with her, so that
I almost drop dead. It must be an unconscious wish that
she should already die. You can imagine the resistance I had
against that idea. She was a childhood love of mine. And,
as a matter of fact, after I worked that through with
Freud—that was in the late, the second part of analysis—
I never again had those dizzy spells.

DR. FREEMAN: How long did you have them?

DR. REIK: For many months. But that was, of course,
the correct interpretation. The fact that I loved her very
much doesn't contradict it. On the contrary, it confirms it.
Otherwise I wouldn't have punished myself.

DR. FREEMAN: But it is quite possible to care for someone and still be angry with them and not have it obliterate
the feelings of affection you have for them.

DR. REIK: Correct. That is perhaps what differentiates
the analyst from other people. He has, so to speak, more
moral courage to face unpleasant thoughts. And it seems to
be a demand of mental hygiene to go to the end with the
thought, not to interrupt it. To go to the end of the
thought, however unpleasant and however contradictory
it might be to your usual aesthetic or ethical values.

You know Rousseau? I never liked him. He had no
temperament. Nothing. He was a man without courage.
Anatole France once called him a *"poisson froid."*

DR. FREEMAN: "A cold fish." You mean he never got
angry?

DR. REIK: No, he had no moral courage. I talked about

this in one of my books. Freud asked me to find out where the phrase comes from *"tuer son Mandarin."* That means "to kill one's Mandarin." He thought it is certainly in Rousseau. But it is not in Rousseau. It is originally in Chateaubriand, and someone, Balzac I think, attributed it to Rousseau by mistake. The fable is: Let's say a man sits in Paris with his students in Mansard. He has nothing to eat and he is cold. But he knows that if he pushes a button, a Mandarin, a high functionary in the Chinese government, will die in Peking and leave him one hundred thousand dollars. What would he do? Would he not push the button?

DR. FREEMAN: What was Chateaubriand's answer?

DR. REIK: Chateaubriand said: "He would not do that."

DR. FREEMAN: I think we would be tempted, but we would not push the button. The next generation would push the button.

DR. REIK: Before they are tempted.

DR. FREEMAN: Remember the reaction some people had to the man who found ten thousand dollars and returned the money? The contempt in which his children held him? His was a moral kind of behavior. I think those children would push the button.

DR. REIK: I think the answer is: today you'd have someone else push the button. And not know what he was doing.

DR. FREEMAN: That shows lack of moral courage. Because if anyone is going to push the button, then at least push it yourself.

DR. REIK: It continues that we are all murderers deep down. It is quite true. So moral courage is partly being able to face unpleasant truths in oneself and in others, too. And then not run away, not to run away. I used the following comparison once: Let's say, there is a man who stands before Tiffany on Fifth Avenue, and sees there a diamond bracelet and he is tempted to throw a stone through the window and to steal that bracelet. Now, he can do the following: He can say: "I shall not do that out of selfish reasons because I would land in jail." or: "I cannot do that because I'll harm these Tiffany people who never did any wrong to me." No? All kinds of reasons why not. But what would you say if this man runs like haunted down Fifth Avenue. That would be the case of repression. He repressed that thought because he was afraid of it. That is not good.

DR. FREEMAN: In other words, the degree or the amount of things repressed is an index of how much moral courage a man has?

DR. REIK: Yes, to a certain extent.

DR. FREEMAN: It is then a question of facing how bad you are, but not acting on it?

DR. REIK: Not "bad."

DR. FREEMAN: I mean "bad" in quotes.

DR. REIK: Yes.

DR. FREEMAN: The existence of negative impulses.

DR. REIK: Yes.

DR. FREEMAN: What should an analyst know and be aware of if his patient has been in analysis with someone else?

DR. REIK: There is a rule that when a person has previously been in analysis, the second analyst has an advantage. Namely, he has the benefit of the first analysis which has brought certain things out. Then he has to analyze the transference of the patient to the first analyst, which is an easier field because he need not go back so quickly to the parents—he could see certain of those things in the transference relationship with the previous analyst.

The second analyst also has the duty to do the direct

opposite of what the first analyst did. For example, if the first analyst talked very much, the second—the new one—should talk very little. If the first one talked very little, the second should talk more. If the first one treated the patient a certain way, he should try to treat the patient the opposite way. That is a rule.

DR. FREEMAN: How would you interview a prospective patient?

DR. REIK: There are certain modifications now. Freud had only one interview. The next time the patient came he explained the basic rule and let the patient lie down. Incidentally, at first he let all patients lie down, but later he came to the recognition that in certain cases it is not indicated. We usually have two interviews now, both with the patient sitting.

In this first interview we have a freedom which we don't have later on. Namely, we have the freedom to ask questions, which later on is almost forbidden. We don't ask questions during analysis. Nor do we answer questions, generally, except if someone going out says: "Where is the next pharmacy?" Oscar Wilde once said: "Questions are never indiscreet. Answers are, sometimes," which is a very good aphorism.

As I mentioned, there are certain criteria for judging the emotional balance of a person. How far is the person able to work without too great inhibitions, procrastination, perfectionism, checking and rechecking, anxieties, and so on? Also how far is the person able to love—not in the narrower sense of sexual love, but generally to love people, his father, his mother, his sister and so on without too great an influx of hositility or hate.

DR. FREEMAN: How would you phrase your question to elicit that information?

DR. REIK: I would say: "How do you rate yourself?" in this direction: "Could you tell me something about . . .?"

Or I often ask the patient simply: "Were you shy? . . .
Are you shy?" And if he says, "Yes," we discuss it. I ask
him: "Does it not depend on the behavior of the other
person with whom you speak? If I behave naturally and
spontaneously and say, 'Come in. Are you shy?' I put you
at your ease. But if I would be pompous or dignified, you
would remain shy, no?"

Another possibility would be to ask a person about fears.
That means we differentiate between a neurotic fear, a
psychotic fear and a normal fear. For instance, when I
walk on Broadway and cross the street and a truck that
I didn't see comes around the corner, I get frightened.
That would be normal. That is a reality fear, I would
say. But there are certain neurotic fears or psychotic fears
which are not normal. I explain that to the patient in consultation during the first interview. I usually illustrate it
by saying: "Assume I sit here in the evening and write.
Suddenly I have the impression that a big snake comes
from the carpet towards me. That would be a psychotic
fear. But if I would sit in the African jungle at night and
in the bushes there is something, that would not be a psychotic fear, that would be a reality fear."

Now, there are other fears. For instance hypochondri-
acal fears. A person is afraid that he has cancer or tuber-
culosis without any objective symptoms. Or he has a little
bruise on the mouth and thinks he will get cancer of the
lip. Or there are neurotic fears in the expectancy of impending calamities. I had a patient who said to me: "I
laugh about the people who are afraid of the H-bomb.
I'm not afraid of the H-bomb. I'm afraid of what could
happen from somewhere without my anticipating it. Illness, death. Something for which I am entirely unprepared."

If you see that this fear is there you would conclude
there is a certain obsessional neurosis. For instance, the

fear of this vague calamity, which has as its foundation a fear of retaliation for murderous thoughts.

DR. FREEMAN: What other freedoms or leeway do we have now as analysts?

DR. REIK: The freedom which Freud didn't have, namely we ask about the sex life of the patient.

DR. FREEMAN: Specifically?

DR. REIK: Specifically. That is possible since analysis and sexual knowledge are now widely spread. This kind of question wasn't possible in the time of Freud. And the fact that it is now is in part due to the influence of psychoanalysis.

For this first interview we break yet another rule. Namely we make notes. But only certain notes—the names and the ages of the person who are nearest to the patient. Let me explain that. It is almost impossible to keep in mind all the names and the age differences between parents and sisters and brothers of all the patients. Freud said that you should ask the names because we unconsciously connect certain ideas with names, whether we want to or not. So that when someone is called, let us say, Jane, we know we have a certain idea connected with the word Jane. And Freud said to me once: "If we don't know the names, the situation is like in certain plays, in which the names of the acting figures are not said but rather called the father, the mother, the uncle, a neighbor, and that gives only a hazy idea of the characters."

DR. FREEMAN: In the first interviews the patient can also ask questions of us.

DR. REIK: Yes. For instance, the patient asks: "How long will it take?" Freud told us: "In general, of course, I circumvent this question, but I have a very good answer for that. I say, 'I cannot tell that until I know more of your case. I have to study your case and your personality —how far you are able to face certain unpleasant truths about yourself and others.'" And he made an interesting comparison. He said: "I once read a fable. An Athenean walked toward Sparta in ancient Greece and when he saw the city from afar, he asked a Spartan peasant working in the meadow, 'Hey, how far is it to Sparta?' And the peasant gave the paradoxical answer, 'Walk.' The answer is not as paradoxical as it seems. It means that when you walk, then I can tell you according to your speed, whether you need half an hour or two hours." Then Freud said: "After telling the patient this story, I tell him I need a certain trial time or test time, the first five, six weeks, and then I could tell how long it will, in my estimation, take to analyze him." In Vienna that meant, of course, daily analysis. Except on Sunday.

By the way, Freud talked jokingly about the "Sunday crust." That means between Saturday and Monday there was forming a certain crust in the attitude of the patient, which you had to scratch off until he came again to the rapport with the analyst and his associations.

DR. FREEMAN: What were the fees in Vienna for six times a week?

DR. REIK: They were very modest compared to American standards.

DR. FREEMAN: Are there any other questions that one should answer. For instance the patient asks about the analyst's training. Did you answer such questions?

DR. REIK: Never. We were not in this situation in Vienna in these times.

DR. FREEMAN: But now they do ask. Often patients come ambivalently. And what they tend to do with their questions are only partly for information, and partly they are an indirect attack.

DR. REIK: Yes. That is already attack, I would say. In general, questions have the character of attack. In literature, the motif which occurs and reoccurs is that a princess or her father, the king, has certain questions to solve, a riddle. Wooers come and want to marry the princess and get the kingdom. But, if they don't solve the riddle, they are killed. For instance, in *Turandot,* which Puccini composed.

DR. FREEMAN: What is the personal relationship between the patient and his analyst?

DR. REIK: As Freud said: "Analysis has to be led in abstinence."

DR. FREEMAN: Does the abstinence resemble in a sense whatever deprivation the child has had . . .

DR. REIK: It means the patient wants to be loved by the analyst, perhaps because of his deprivations as a child. I remember I had a woman patient—I was much younger, that was twenty years ago—who got up from the couch and ran out. It was because I didn't want to have sexual intercourse with her. She came back then in ten minutes.

DR. FREEMAN: Did she really expect this from you?

DR. REIK: Yes. First she wanted me to lie down with her . . .

DR. FREEMAN: If a patient makes a direct request of this kind . . .

DR. REIK: No, no, ours is a nobler task.

DR. FREEMAN: Did you just say: "No, there are other things to do," or did you interpret why she wanted this?

DR. REIK: Yes, we traced it back from childhood.

DR. FREEMAN: And this is one of the points at which you would interpret?

DR. REIK: Right. I once said to a patient: "Our aim here is that you shouldn't want Mr. Reik, but Mr. Right." There are, of course, certain temperaments, especially in women, who would not be satisfied with that. I remember Freud told me once that there are certain types of women who are *vitrioleuses.* But Freud also said that you have to repeat the frustration which the patient had as a child in his insatiable thirst for love. And then let him go beyond that, you know.

DR. FREEMAN: Assuming the child's need for love is insatiable, shouldn't there be some measure of fulfillment —a small measure—not as much as it wants, but enough to keep the child growing.

DR. REIK: You are friendly to the patient, you show interest in his welfare, no? That's enough. After all, a patient is also entitled to a certain amount of counter-transference, of interest in her welfare. You cannot remain a cold fish the way many analysts trained by the New York psychoanalytic do. It is incredible. My daughter was in analysis and gave her analyst a book for Christmas and the analyst said: "Why did you give me that book?" and did not accept it. It is inhuman.

DR. FREEMAN: If a patient gives a gift, doesn't that invite the analyst to give a gift also?

DR. REIK: Yes, so what? I met Freud in the street in Vienna and he said: "What a nuisance this is. A patient gave me a book and now I have to look for a book to give him." In other words you could accept a small gift, and thank the patient and also get his associations, as well.

DR. FREEMAN: Earlier you mentioned asking a patient if he was shy. What are some of the causes of shyness?

DR. REIK: Shyness is that you project the feeling of self-criticism or self-hate onto your surroundings. Then it comes back, and you feel shy. There is a shortcut to overcome shyness and that is merely to say: "I'm shy." I said that when I gave my first lecture in Leiden, in Holland. I said to the audience in the beginning: "I'm shy to speak in a foreign language." I was in the lecture hall at the university and I was very impressed with that, too, and so in the first moments I felt shy. But I overcame it after I had admitted it. When you go into a social gathering and say you are shy, you will overcome it.

DR. FREEMAN: Simply by saying so? Because you've expressed it, or because it becomes accepted by the others?

DR. REIK: You have expressed it, and at the same time you have captured, so to speak, the benevolence of the audience. They feel nicer towards you.

DR. FREEMAN: Is there the possibility that some people are afraid to admit their shyness because they are afraid of capturing antagonism or ridicule?

DR. REIK: Then it is because they themselves feel antagonism or ridicule towards the audience.

Freud reproached me when I first spoke before the Psychoanalytic Society for talking down to them. I must have been so shy that I tried to overcome it, you know? My daughter, in fact, has the same counter-phobic tendency. She has a fear of examinations, and whenever an examination is announced, she is the first to get to it, to want to do it. She's so afraid that she goes forward. Anna Freud calls it "Flag Forward."

There is a philosopher whom I like, Emerson. He said always do that of which you are most afraid in life. I would subtly encourage a patient to do that which he is afraid of. Goethe is a good example of that. He was afraid of heights, of falling down. You know what that means? A feminine tendency—a fallen woman. It was a great feminine tendency of his. But he forced himself to go up in the Muenchdorf Strassburg—which in those days was like the Empire State Building today—and stand there on the platform. He forced himself every day, and he stood there and stood there. That is a counter-phobic reaction.

DR. FREEMAN: If a woman is afraid of falling, that is generally unexceptional, because she is feminine? But is the real reason unconscious?

DR. REIK: The fear is conscious. The reason is unconscious.

DR. FREEMAN: In other words it is symbolic.

DR. REIK: Yes, it's symbolic. *I fall for him*—to be a fallen woman. In Vienna the idea was passed on from mother to daughter that the first duty of a girl is to keep her skirts down.

DR. FREEMAN: What would you say is at the root of the fear, for instance, of school examinations?

DR. REIK: It's generally man's fear, because he could fall, he could fail. It means a test of his masculinity. Consciously it is the fear of social or professional failure. Unconsciously, of course, to fail means that his penis will fall; that he will not pass his test as a male. Also in slang they say: "He makes a pass at a girl."

DR. FREEMAN: And with a woman?

DR. REIK: With a woman it could be the same thing, it could be she is afraid she's not a virgin. The fear is irrational. It has something to do with masturbation, you know? Women sometimes have the fear that they are not a virgin if they have penetrated their hand in touching themselves.

DR. FREEMAN: Unconsciously?

DR. REIK: Unconsciously. I remember a patient who was married and finally got pregnant. Then she went from one gynecologist to another because she was afraid she would have a malformed child. During the analysis that fear led back to the forgotten fear that she had ruined herself because she had masturbated as a young girl. Consequently she thought the child would be born with one leg, or one arm, or such.

DR. FREEMAN: The reason for this feeling of guilt about masturbation, is it always unconscious?

DR. REIK: It is unconscious, because people don't remember that they were warned against it. They don't remember, let us say, that mother said to them: "Take the thumb out of your mouth"—thumbsucking or such is a displacement. Or: "Don't play with your hair." Girls play with their hair.

DR. FREEMAN: I'm thinking of one patient who remembers when she was little—she had a girlfriend that she used to go to the movies with. And one day, she and her girlfriend, who was older than she, were lying on her bed, and they must have been mutually masturbating. Then this patient's mother came into the room—

DR. REIK:—and saw them, caught them—

DR. FREEMAN: Yes, but the mother had no negative reaction at all. The patient said their guilt made them stop. And I said: "What did your mother say?" And she said: "My mother said to me, 'What are you doing?' Not in any offensive way. And I told her, 'Nothing!' " I asked: "Did your mother know what was going on? Were you afraid of what might happen?" And she said: "No, because there was something about her which wasn't punitive." And then the patient said that later on she was in the living room and her mother was being visited by a lady friend of hers. And the patient heard her mother saying about her, laughingly, as though it were some kind of a joke: "I guess she's exploring new experiences."

DR. REIK: Yes, but this is an exceptional mother. Most people forget that they were asked: "What are you doing?" And a grown-up person who is very embarrassed or angry whenever someone asks: "What are you doing?" always connects it with masturbation. I once saw a cartoon in which a mother says to the governess: "Go see what Peggy's doing in the garden and tell her she 'must not.' " In other words, whatever she does is wrong.

DR. FREEMAN: But the sense of guilt stems only from the introjection of the parents saying, "Don't!"

DR. REIK: The sense of guilt comes, without exception,

from the *violent feeling* that is a reaction to being told, "Don't."

DR. FREEMAN: Only from the violent feeling? Not from the sexual behavior itself?

DR. REIK: No. Not from the sexual behavior but from the violent feeling which is really there when a parent says, "Don't" or when the child *imagines* that the parents would say, "Don't."

DR. FREEMAN: Then it is a projection of the superego? In other words, the child assumes that somebody else would say, "Don't," and then objects, gets angry at the possibility.

DR. REIK: Yes, and then comes the reaction.

DR. FREEMAN: Because of his own superego?

DR. REIK: Not at this time—

DR. FREEMAN: At what point can you call it superego?

DR. REIK: The introjection of the parents?

DR. FREEMAN: Yes. At what age?

DR. REIK: Four or five. Melanie Klein thinks that the superego is already formed before three. That's the difference between her and Anna Freud.

DR. FREEMAN: Would that not also depend to some degree upon the native intelligence of the child? And upon the developmental. . . .

DR. REIK: Maturity, yes. If the child is intelligent enough to understand what's going on at a younger age, then the process would start earlier.

DR. FREEMAN: Would the introjection be a rational, conscious process, or would it be an instinctual process?

DR. REIK: In the beginning it's an automatic process. Later on you introject consciously.

DR. FREEMAN: Yes, but if it's automatic, in order for it to be introjected, does it first have to be understood?

DR. REIK: No, it could be automatic, it need not be understood.

DR. FREEMAN: You mean instinctive—the child simply responds to the tone?

DR. REIK: Yes. Just as a baby responds or a dog reacts to the tone.

DR. FREEMAN: So the superego could form even at a pre-verbal level?

DR. REIK: Yes.

DR. FREEMAN: When the communication is only the tone of the voice.

DR. REIK: Yes, the tone of the voice.

DR. FREEMAN: What else would you say we are taught at a pre-verbal level?

DR. REIK: To be afraid, to hope, to lose hope. For instance, you know the sickness they call marasmus. When the infant has no one to love it, it becomes hopeless and sometimes even dies. Also, you know a certain part of the communication between analyst and patient is pre-verbal. One unconscious understands the other unconscious without words.

DR. FREEMAN: What about non-verbal communications, as differentiated from pre-verbal?

DR. REIK: That happens often; if you live together with someone for a long time you understand each other by glances. Or when women cannot talk to each other because there are men around, they look at each other and understand.

DR. FREEMAN: What about men?

DR. REIK: Men don't understand each other very much.

DR. FREEMAN: And men with women?

DR. REIK: Men with women could understand.

DR. FREEMAN: Then men don't generally communicate with each other?

DR. REIK: Not in conspiratorial whispers, as women do.

DR. FREEMAN: Does that tend to isolate them more than women?

DR. REIK: Certainly, certainly, they are islands, each one. Women, they say, are sisters under the skin. On the other hand, you could say, if Dr. Sulzberger is correct, there are certain remnants of mistrust of the other woman, whoever she is.

DR. FREEMAN: Does that stem from the original distrust of the mother?

DR. REIK: Yes. There is a certain mistrust among women, even if they are friends.

DR. FREEMAN: I think there are some women who are friends because they *don't* trust each other.

DR. REIK: Yes, it's safer to keep them in your gunsight.

DR. FREEMAN: A patient's husband demands that she produce, work, and when she asked what would happen if she stopped and only kept house, he answered: "Then there'd be a divorce in one month, because I didn't marry just another schnooky housewife."

DR. REIK: Of course, the demand to produce is a projection of a man's unrest onto his wife—his own dissatisfaction.

DR. FREEMAN: Is there not then a kind of resistance to producing, if one is expected to produce to earn one's love?

DR. REIK: It is the same in general. But a child is a production, it is the greatest production one can have. The other is a peculiarity of his which showed that he was dissatisfied with himself and projected it on the patient.

DR. FREEMAN: But when a child feels that in order to be accepted by the parent it has to be something special, what is the dynamic?

DR. REIK: There are such cases. And the dynamic is that of an early guilt feeling in the child. It is an interesting problem. I will give you an instance. I treat a man

who is thirty-nine, and a writer. His sexual life is masochistic. He licks women and lets himself be masturbated.
He has intercourse only out of duty, and finally he produced a child. I helped him to be able to have sexual intercourse normally with women, whether his wife or not. He
can now, with other women, not his wife. I said to him:
"I don't give a damn with whom you had your intercourse last, with your wife or with a prostitute, but I
want to bring about that you can have it." And he did,
with no relapses into his masochism. Now about this man,
we discovered that as a little boy he wanted to be liked.
He always thought he was not liked, not acknowledged,
and now he blossoms because everyone invites him to produce for them. He is liked. That helps him. Now the
pathology is the following: He must have been right—
that he wasn't liked as a boy. That interests me. Why
wasn't he liked? Now he behaves wonderfully socially,
but as a boy, perhaps, he made himself objectionable.
Why? Because he felt guilty, early. He felt guilty because he wanted to kill his father.

What also interests me here is an idea I flirt with, that
is the Dreyfus case. That a Jew at that time, when the
French were so anti-Semitic, wants to become an officer
and is so full of patriotism as he is—that when these
people thought he was a traitor, he thought they must
somehow be right. Namely, unconsciously, he didn't give
a damn about France, as a patriot. He wanted to be liked,
just as my patient wants to be liked. He wanted to be
accepted by the bourgeoisie. Now, the strange thing is that
no one liked Dreyfus. Not even those who entered into
the fight for him, such as Emile Zola, Anatole France.
Everybody said he was an objectionable person. Dreyfus
maintained his innocence, and he was eventually found
not guilty of the spying they accused him of. I don't
know anything about his family life, but unconsciously

he felt guilty for wanting to be loved. What helped him, and that was his pathology, was that he could always sleep. He could sit down and sleep for hours. I would like to write a book with the title, *Alfred Dreyfus, the Jewish Masochist.*

The pathology of childhood is interesting. This patient of mine wanted to be liked. The interesting thing is he was an Eastern Jew, converted to Catholicism. Now he has nothing to do with it anymore. But for a time he was a Catholic. He was too naive to understand why. He went to confession. He confessed and satisfied his masochism.

DR. FREEMAN: About the girl I mentioned. Is that the same kind of pathology, her feeling of not being accepted? That she wanted to kill her mother?

DR. REIK: No, it is not the same. I don't think so.

DR. FREEMAN: Isn't the parallel that if the boy wants to kill his father and so he feels guilty, ergo, the girl wants to kill her mother and so she feels guilty?

DR. REIK: No. There is another thing which is very interesting with girls. I had such a patient who had the idea that the marriage between her parents was very noisy and full of scandals. She had the idea that the father does something cruel to mother, because in the night she heard noises in the bedroom. And she thought sexual intercourse is something which a father does to mother. And in the morning at breakfast she always looked at her mother and at her father to see whether mother is sad, whether she is worried or has pains, because she thought when she heard the noises there was a quarrel or a fight.

DR. FREEMAN: Is there a possibility, then, in the origin of guilt feelings in the girl, that the girl too wants to kill her father?

DR. REIK: That would be a reversed Oedipus situation, to a later time.

DR. FREEMAN: Yes, since the first love object of the girl is the mother, and her assumption is that the father is violating the mother, hurting her. That makes her want to kill him—not for the same reason that a boy wants to kill his father, though the result would be the same.

DR. REIK: Right, right. The origin of guilt feeling is murder.

DR. FREEMAN: But it need not be towards persons of the same sex.

DR. REIK: It need not be, in the case of girls.

DR. FREEMAN: What if it is? Would that be more likely to remain as a guilt feeling, if she wants to kill her mother rather than if she wants to kill her father?

DR. REIK: Yes, I would say.

DR. FREEMAN: Because if she wants to kill her father, then in a sense she is combating the Oedipus complex already. But if she wants to kill her mother?

DR. REIK: It would be a stronger feeling of guilt.

DR. FREEMAN: And that might be one of the seeds of her own homosexuality?

DR. REIK: Right. Because it would be the case of Electra, who, though she didn't kill her mother, got her brother to do it for her.

DR. FREEMAN: What does the analyst do if a patient asks for an explanation—the patient says: "I don't know why I'm nervous or why I'm upset."

DR. REIK: Silence.

DR. FREEMAN: Fine. How long should the silence take? Supposing the patient tries to associate and can come up with nothing. And finally he says: "What do you think? What could it be? I've got a blank mind."

DR. REIK: One of my patients said: "Here we are, two

minds without a single thought." And he was making fun of me, too, in that. But the thing is the patient must simply say what is in his mind.

DR. FREEMAN: When is the best time to interpret?

DR. REIK: Ordinarily you don't interpet immediately when you know something. You postpone it.

Freud emphasized that before you make any interpretation in depth you must make the patient understand what is the difference between conscious, unconscious, and the repressed unconscious and thoughts. Such an introduction appears to be necessary. Freud also turned our attention to the fact that all repressions come from outside us, were imposed on us. Let me explain what he meant. When you were a little girl, your father or mother always told you you should look to the right and to the left and wait until no car comes before you cross the street. Now you do that automatically before you cross the street and you don't think each time that your mother warned you in that way. It became an inner acquisition. It is exactly the same with repressions.

Also sometimes the resistance is such that it won't let the patient accept an obvious fact. He may even acknowledge the truth intellectually but he's not yet ready to accept it as being part of him. If you would tell a patient who is quite unprepared that he hates his father, he would think that you are crazy.

That reminds me, we had a professor of dermatology in Vienna, an old professor. He specialized in treating syphilis. Once a woman, an aristocrat, came with her seventeen-year-old daughter. And he examined the girl and called the mother in. He said: "Countess, I'm sorry to say your daughter has syphilis." The mother said: "Impossible. My daughter has never seen a man. She was educated in Sacré Coeur. She never had anything to do with a man." The professor said: "But it is so, you can believe me." Then after a long hesitation the mother said: "Is it possible that she caught it on the toilet?" He said: "Yes, it is possible, but uncomfortable."

DR. FREEMAN: Is wit another way of hiding the truth? In other words, when you say something funny then . . .

DR. REIK: But not in analysis. You can laugh with the patient, but not about the patient. I give you a very little piece of observation. I treated a young man, and after the first hours he began to tell me funny stories. I laughed and laughed and laughed. I was very amused, until I found out that was his purpose. He wanted to amuse me. He didn't talk about himself. He talked about all kinds of things. Funny stories from here and there. That was his kind of resistance.

DR. FREEMAN: What did you do?

DR. REIK: I told him: "I don't want to hear the stories." I give you an example of that technique. My colleague treats a man who is a plumber. This plumber works in Brooklyn and the analyst is in Manhattan. So the patient always begins the hour with "why I came late." The traffic jam there on the highway from Queens, and he had to wait and couldn't help it. Then he begins about pipes— what his customer said about the pipes so, and the pipes so, and that takes half an hour. And after that he is so tired, he falls asleep. That is the last five minutes. So the colleague asked my advice, what should he do, and I said to him: "Tell him he has the liberty to talk about whatever he wants, except two things—the traffic jams and the pipes." That amounts to "don't."

DR. FREEMAN: How does this coincide with the original instruction, that the patient must say everything that comes to his mind?

DR. REIK: But that was resistance. I give you an instance. I had a patient at the time who did not talk about his childhood. It seems he didn't want to remember. I told

Freud this. He said: "A man who does not like to think of his past is a ne'er-do-well." I wanted to object to that. Then I realized that he was right. There must be certain psycho-pathological consequences for a man who breaks off all bridges to the past. So you see what it is and overcome it.

I give you another instance which is very interesting. More than forty years ago, a professor of dermatology at Vienna University came to me for analysis. He was fifty-six, and he complained that whenever he examines women now, especially attractive women, he gets an erection. At this time, there was a so-called "Salon Rock," a very long jacket. He wore this besides his doctor's coat so he could conceal the erection. And he wants to get rid of that problem. He cannot stand it any longer or he'll have to give up his practice. So he began his analysis. After a few weeks he brought me a book. Then he brought me a box of cigarettes and at another time he brought me bonbons, and so on. I didn't get it. What was the matter with this man? In the analysis, he talked a little bit about a younger brother whom he admired very much. I went to Freud, because I didn't know what to do with this man and Freud said: "He's a homosexual unconsciously. He is in love with his brother and you represent his brother." The brother was twenty years younger than he. And the other problem was an alibi.

Freud on this occasion told me a little anecdote of de Maupassant's. There is a young aristocrat who had an affair with a married woman. And her husband slowly gets suspicious. At certain hours the husband is away and he is suspicious of his young wife. The young man heard about it and he makes a fine plan. He goes to the Opéra Comique in Paris and pays court to a ballerina. He goes with her to dinner, he goes to the theater and to the balls with her and within a few weeks all of Paris was saying that he was having an affair with this ballet dancer. The story is called "The Alibi." And Freud said: "So this patient has an alibi with his over-activities and over-attraction towards women. He wants to hide from himself his love for his younger brother."

DR. FREEMAN: What do you do when you discover in a person who thinks himself normal, that there is homosexuality very close to the surface. For example, a patient told me a dream: "In the dream," the patient said, "there were goldfish all over me, and I wasn't afraid of them. I just picked them up and threw them back into the fishbowl. I could even put them into my mouth and spit them back into the fishbowl. I was surprised and pleased with myself that I could do this and not be afraid. But suddenly the last fish started to wriggle around and I couldn't get hold of it. I got terrified, and I woke up scared stiff."

DR. REIK: That is a transparent dream.

If you allow me I shall read you something: "The woman stood beside me looking at the man preparing his fishing tackle and said, 'Poor fish.' Then I asked her, 'Why are there so many fishermen and so few fisherwomen?' 'Well, because it is a man's sport.' Then she added 'Women perhaps don't like to touch live fish.'

"Walking along, I thought that we use the phrase regarding women: 'They fish for compliments.' Do they not throw out alluring and tempting bait for us men to swallow? And then they keep us helplessly and deliciously dangling. And then after a long time we poor fish are taken off the hook and put into the safe box of married life, no longer to enjoy the adventures of freedom. Why are there so few fisherwomen? Is it because fishing is a silent and lonely sport? Women like to be in company and like to talk. When that woman said: 'Poor fish,' it was perhaps not because she felt sorry for the fish, but for us men who are snared by the bait. Women of course do their fishing in society and have no need for the sport itself. A bikini swim suit worn by a young girl is much more seductive bait than a worm. Two hours later, I sat in the dining room in the hotel and observed how the young women scanned the men as they were entering the hall. It was as if they were looking through the glass walls of an aquarium. 'Poor fish,' I thought again."

DR. FREEMAN: I thought that there was a connection with the male genitals.

DR. REIK: Yes, the fish is, of course, a penis symbol. What this man dreamed is, of course, homosexual. He even takes a fish into his mouth. You know what a patient of mine told me—it reminded me now when you spoke. He came home very late at night and near the park in Riverside Drive three sailors came at him. They beat him and forced him to kneel down and to suck them off, all three. Your patient speaks directly from . . . He says the fish wriggles.

DR. FREEMAN: But until then he wasn't afraid because he threw the others back in the bowl.

DR. REIK: Yes, he threw them away. Even from the mouth. You could say that during the dream the homosexual temptation became strong, which made him afraid. It became stronger and the reaction of fear amounts to: "No, I don't want that." You have to interpet that.

DR. FREEMAN: I think it is too soon.

DR. REIK: I thought he's been with you a long time.

DR. FREEMAN: No. He feels it is a long time and once said so. So I asked him how long did he think he had been with me and he said: "It must be a year or two." But he has only been with me for four months.

DR. REIK: How often?

DR. FREEMAN: Three times a week.

DR. REIK: If there is a next occasion in which you feel that the homosexual theme is near the surface, then remind him of the dream. Because if it is true that he re-presses the homosexuality so strongly, then he must have some hostility to women. But only interpret it when it comes much nearer to the surface, and things are much clearer to him about homosexuality. And point out that he says "no" to homosexuality in that dream.

There are many men who are afraid of homosexuality. I had such a case yesterday in control analysis. You say: "You are no more homosexual than I am." This fear of homosexuality is quite exaggerated. He is not really homo-sexual. It is as if a horse shies away from his own shadow in the sun. Everybody has a certain homosexuality. If the fear is too exaggerated, then he is not. So the pathological fear is there. The homosexuality is not pathological, but the fear is pathological.

DR. FREEMAN: What if the homosexuality is the pathology?

DR. REIK: Then he would not function sexually in a normal way. But the dermatologist I was telling you about was also going through a change of life. He was fifty-six. Freud said: "Break off the analysis and tell him it is better if he goes to a professor who gives him hormones, middle-age hormones."

DR. FREEMAN: When you say function normally sexually, how do you mean that?

DR. REIK: I shall explain that. There are three criteria. One is: when a man has his orgasm, where is the sensation? I ask them, in the second or third interview. On the tip of the penis or near the testicles? It should be at the tip. Because if you knife someone the experience should be here—think of it as a knife, the center of gravity should be at the tip. If a man begins analysis when it is near the testic'es, which would correspond anatomically much more to the vagina, in analysis it should move to the front.

Also, there is too great a focus in everybody's attitude

on the sex need of the man. The man should take care of the woman; that means that he considers her. She is slower to be aroused than he is. The arousal process is different. She is, so to speak, a phase difference behind, slower, which he has to consider. But then there comes a point of no return for the man. If this point is reached, he should not take the slightest consideration of the woman. He should go ahead, selfishly. And in doing that he would also give more pleasure to the woman, because if he would now artificially consider her, he would have a very weak orgasm. It would be like urinating, without sensation.

The third is that the normal orgasm should have the character of an eruption. Like a volcano—an explosion—and not the feeling that it just "flowed out." Those are the three criteria.

With the woman it is, of course, a question of whether it is the clitoris or the vagina. There is a difference in character between the clitoral excitement and the genital excitement. The clitoris corresponds biologically to a little penis. The excitement of the clitoris is like the ticking of a clock—that is the sensation. The vaginal orgasm is deep down and is like the opening and closing of a fist. Involuntary spasms and many, not one, repeated like muscle contractions. One must ask her, did she reach an orgasm at all? Many don't and you have to explain that to them; that the reason was not his selfishness, but the height of his passion. That should please a normal woman. Of course, eventually he should bring her to an orgasm also.

DR. FREEMAN: Are there any kinds of memories among patients which they have in common, or dreams which are similar?

DR. REIK: It happens sometimes. I'll give you an instance. Sometimes a memory is connected with a dream. A patient of mine dreamed that he goes with his mother to Prospect Park and in that park he sees on the other side something which interests him. But there is a fence and in the fence there is a hole, and he wants to go through this hole but he thinks: "Perhaps I am too small." And then he thinks again: "If I go through this hole perhaps I would be electrocuted." Now, that is a clear incestuous dream. The fence: the mother. And he remembers that, first, he really went with his mother to Prospect Park, and second, that he saw his mother nude on the toilet. Then comes, of course, the fear of punishment, castration, if he were to go through the hole.

Dr. Freeman: Are there any memories which are easier for patients to remember than others?

Dr. Reik: Yes, easier to remember are those which are not connected with repressed material.

Dr. Freeman: What do you think of the technique of going right to whatever pathology the patient's productions suggest, rather than the way we have been trained, to go slowly layer by layer? My feeling is that if the patient can already translate the underlying pathology, not only is he ready to discuss it but somewhere within him he knows what he is doing and that if the analyst does not pick it up, the patient might misinterpret it to mean that the analyst, too, is afraid of the pathology and that, therefore, he, the patient, has reason indeed to fear it.

Dr. Reik: Good. But I shall sober you. Freud told me that the danger of a young analyst is that he wants to penetrate the core of a neurosis *as soon as possible*. And he warned me against that. It reminds me of a story I read the other day.

In the Napoleonic War a certain situation developed and Napoleon called his staff together. All the generals sat around the table and asked what should be done to change the situation. And the oldest general said: "The most urgent thing in this situation is to wait." That's wonderful.

DR. FREEMAN: When do you interpret the negative transference?

DR. REIK: When it has developed enough so that it is clear.

DR. FREEMAN: Isn't there a danger of losing the patient if you wait too long?

DR REIK: Certainly. Transference can sometimes be a sensitive problem. When I started in analytic practice, there was no such thing as supervision. But I knew that Freud walked on the Ringstrasse, so I waited for him there and accompanied him on his walks and told him of my patients. One of my first cases was a young girl. And in six months of analysis—and that meant in Vienna six times a week—she never showed the slightest interest in me, personally. There was no transference. And I asked Freud about it. He said to me: "I give you this advice; make her jealous!" which is certainly unorthodox. You see Freud did not correspond to the image Americans have of him that he was dogmatic.

I had a big waiting room and this young girl was there waiting for me, and another patient—a girl patient—came out, so I touched the second patient's shoulder and said, "I was very glad to see you, Ida." Very friendly to the girl who left. And the first patient came in then, and you should have heard her! She said: "What has this blonde hussy got that I haven't got?" And then she said: "Your mother must have been a she-dog," and such things, you know? And she abused me for a half an hour. That is what Freud had tried to say. It was good insofar as it brought all the emotions out.

DR. FREEMAN: What kind of transference remarks does one expect from a patient?

DR. REIK: Very often there will be no remarks at all.

But I will give you some instances of behavior which indicate various transference attitudes.

There was a Rumanian girl who was one of my first patients, and she always told me that the taxi driver with whom she drove from her hotel to my office took a long detour to make money. I had no idea what that meant. Then Freud told me that she was suspicious that I prolong the treatment in order to get more money out of her, which was her way of showing negative transference.

I give you another instance. I treated a young man, who was at the time a student of Auer, the violin virtuoso, in Vienna. He always came from his lesson with Auer, and brought his violin in the case with him. When he came into my office, he put the violin case on the writings on my desk. Freud, to whom I had told this, said: "Of course, that's an expression of contempt. How much does he pay Auer?" And I asked the patient that. Then Freud said I should charge him at least one crown more than Auer charged him. That was good advice and that stopped his contemptuous attitude towards me.

I'll give you another example of negative transference but this one is coupled with resistance, or, I would say, is the reason for the resistance. I have an analyst under supervision. The patient, a girl, whom this analyst treated, had something against her and the analyst could not find out what the resistance was. I asked her: "Did your patient never say anything critical about your dress, and did she never say anything about your hairdo, and so on?" "No, never." But I nevertheless got the impression that the girl had a negative transference to this analyst, had something against her. But she said the patient denies it. I said: "You must tell her, 'You have something against me.'" And still the patient denied it. Until once she said to the analyst: "When I left yesterday, I thought about you and I thought, 'I know you work seven hours a day. I know you want to get your Ph.D. I know you are not married.' And I suddenly thought, 'Oh, God, I hope I don't get to be like her.'" That's enough of a negative transference, I should say.

DR. FREEMAN: How soon can one reasonably expect a patient to make remarks towards the analyst that indicate the transference?

DR. REIK: When you start analysis. In free association, it begins very early. I remember when I arrived in this country from Holland, I had no money. All my money and what I earned in Vienna was taken by Hitler. The first patient I had in America was a society girl. I don't know how she came to me. Her great worry was whether she should go to Twenty-One, or the Stork Club. So it began. And then she looked around my office and said: "It's very shabby here," which it was, of course. She was accustomed to very luxurious surroundings wherever she went. But that was, of course, the first expression of a negative transference, because one doesn't ordinarily say such things to someone else, especially a girl with her kind of upbringing.

DR. FREEMAN: What kinds of things did you say when you interpreted transference?

DR. REIK: The positive transference you never interpret at all. Only when it turns negative. The positive transference is the waterfall which drives the mill. Why should you interpret that?

DR. FREEMAN: What kind of thing then do you say when you are interpreting the negative transference? When the negative transference is long enough and far enough gone so that it is established, but not so far gone that the patient has left because of it.

DR. REIK: You have to find out what is the nature of this negative transference. I remember a patient in Holland who for many hours accused me of all kinds of stupid things I did, and wrong things I said, and wrong interpretations and how badly I treated her. At a certain point, I interrupted her and said: "Good. Now that you have told me that, tell me how much you like me." I turned it around. That could also be. They could go into a negative transference in order to avoid the positive.

DR. FREEMAN: How does transference develop in cases of obsessional neurotics?

DR. REIK: An obsessional neurotic could come into this room and say: "How should I go to the couch, this way around or this way around?" In the depth it is always the same. It is always the question: "Do I hate or do I love?" That is the original question. So, of course, you also come into this framework of the obsession.

DR. FREEMAN: Is it true that the obsessional does not transfer as much?

DR. REIK: Not as strongly, no.

DR. FREEMAN: Suppose a patient, while in analysis, falls in love with somebody who may or may not be appropriate.

DR. REIK: So we postpone, if possible, the decision, till the end of the analysis.

DR. FREEMAN: What happens to that part of the transference? Is it simply displaced on the other person?

DR. REIK: That could be. It happens sometimes that it is displaced to another person. So the principle is that during analysis you don't make any vital decisions. Neither do you give up a profession, for instance, or let yourself divorce, or get married. Freud always said that should be postponed until we gain insight and maturity with the end of analysis.

There is a man who is in supervision. He has a psychologist in analysis, and this psychologist wants to discuss analysis—the theories. And that is, of course, a resistance. And I told him he should say to his patient: "Look here, analysis is emotional thoughts, not intellectual. But I can promise you someth:ng. After you have finished your analysis successfully—the therapeutic analysis—if you invite me, I shall go down with you and have coffee with you, and we shall discuss analytic theory for hours." It's as you say to a child; "You don't understand it now, not yet, but later on when you are more grown up I will explain it to you." You postpone.

It reminds me of a little anecdote. When Mozart was thirteen, already acknowledged and renowned, a little boy came to him and asked whether he could play the piano for him. Mozart said, "Yes," and he listened. When the little boy finished playing, he asked whether he should become a child prodigy. Mozart said, "No," And the boy said: "But you played before the Empress Maria Theresa in Vienna when you were only six." And Mozart answered: "Yes, but I didn't ask anybody." Quite true, no? In contrast to him, Beethoven was very, very rude. He said to a man who played for him: "You will have to study for two more years before you'll recognize that you have no talent whatsoever."

DR. FREEMAN: When the analyst does intervene during a patient's free association, is he addressing himself to the conscious or the unconscious?

DR. REIK: To the conscious, generally. Sometimes the unconscious.

DR. FREEMAN: Does it frighten a patient, if he's talking about something and you address yourself to his unconscious?

DR. REIK: Sometimes. But when it succeeds, it penetrates like the sound of a clear bell. When you reveal something he repressed and the patient laughs, it is a good

Theodor Reik at Vienna
University, 1912, soon
after he received his
doctorate. The book in
his hand is his doctoral
dissertation, *Flaubert and
"The Temptation of
St. Anthony."*

Theodor Reik (lower left corner) with his
Hungarian cavalry unit in the Austro-Hungarian
Army, 1915.

Dr. Reik with his first wife and their son Arthur at
Bad Wildungen, Austria, 1928.

sign that he has accepted it in this form. It means that he has understood, unconsciously, at least.

DR. FREEMAN: But by the same token, if the response is anger?

DR. REIK: Then it's a resistance. You have to wait out the resistance.

DR. FREEMAN: In other words if he says: "I don't know what you're talking about! We weren't talking about that at all, we were talking about this and that," that means. . . .

DR. REIK: Rejection.

DR. FREEMAN: And against the rejection it did not penetrate?

DR. REIK: Yes, it is resistance. Freud said that a mistake which he always found with analysts is that they speak about the resistance of the repressed. The repressed does not resist. The repressed wants to come out! It is the conscious which has resistance, or the pre-conscious.

DR. FREEMAN: So that the dynamics of the forces of that resistance are what is keeping the repressed material repressed.

DR. REIK: That's right. The repressed material itself wants to come out! And it does come out in free association.

DR. FREEMAN: In other words, something had been done to the repressed material; it did not get repressed of it's own volition.

DR. REIK: Yes, it was, so to speak, forcefully thrown out.

DR. FREEMAN: And the energy or the dynamic is from another source, and that source . . .

DR. REIK: The ego, or the superego, if you want.

DR FREEMAN: Working in conjunction with each other. So that if you hit home—when a patient is ready to accept it—with a restatement of what he already knows, but in terms that he can recognize—that then would be interpretation. But if, when he's talking about one thing, you make a statement directly to what *you* think he is talking about in his subsconscious, and he laughs—it means another connection has been established.

DR. REIK: Yes, yes, certainly.

DR. FREEMAN: Will that help?

DR. REIK: Certainly. That's analysis, and it should help. Even though at the moment he goes on with what he was saying, it pierces some of the resistance.

DR. FREEMAN: Every so often I get a response like: "What are you talking about? How did you get such an idea?" For instance, one patient kept saying "successful" and I kept hearing "succulent" and finally I said, "Say the word loud,' and he said "successful." And I said to myself: "Why would I think—even though he mumbled—why 'succulent'?" So I said to him: "What do you associate with 'succulent'?" He got very angry and said: "Where did you get that from? I didn't say that, did I?" I said: "I didn't say you said it. I only asked you what you associated with it." It must have been close enough that even though he kept saying "successful" I kept hearing "succulent."

DR. REIK: Yes, the repressed material.

DR. FREEMAN: He must have meant something similar to this.

DR. REIK: Certainly.

DR. FREEMAN: This same patient said that all people in analysis are depraved, and I said, "Why?" He said: "Because they are! It's very sad." And I said: "What does depraved mean?" He answered: "Depraved means that you never had what you wanted, you had to starve when you were small, your parents didn't love you." I said: "Will you spell it for me?" He spelled it "depraved." And I said, "What do you associate with the word 'deprived'?"

He said: "Deprived? Sinful. Ugly." And in effect, he defined *depraved*.

DR. REIK: Yes, the opposite.

DR. FREEMAN: So I said: "Do you know which word means which?" He said "No."

DR. REIK: The dictionary . . .

DR. FREEMAN: I did, but I wanted to get his own association. What finally happened was: as he kept talking he was a child who, because he was deprived of love, decided he was an evil, wicked, terrible thing and deserved all the punishment he got from his parents; and he felt depraved. Consequently, thereafter he could only think of a human being who has needs, whose needs are not fulfilled, as depraved, because he had defined it for himself: the kind of person who needs things and who is not given what he needs is by definition depraved. Sad, isn't it?

🙥

DR. FREEMAN: I wanted to ask you about time limits. There was one patient with whom I did an experiment because I accepted him on a time limit. He had only two months. It turned out there was a massive job that had to be done on him so that he wouldn't fall apart, so that he would still function, and if possible, grow. I thought I knew what I was doing, but sometimes . . . Well, the only analogy I can think of is, if someone jumps into the water and you jump in to rescue him because he can't swim, but he struggles so much that he pulls you under. What happened in this case, I think, is that I was pulled under, but I sensed the direction to the other side of the lake, so that even while I was under I kept in the direction which I had sensed.

DR. REIK: . . . The shore . . .

DR. FREEMAN: Yes. And finally, I came up and it

turned out it was the right direction. There is a saying
that we must have a plan for a patient. But I don't always
know where the other side is, but I think I know how to
get there, that is, approximately. And then the patient's
own resistance in the struggle comes up, and it seems for a
moment that I lose the usual way, I only know the
approximate goal.

DR. REIK: I go beyond that even. I used this comparison in a seminar: I compared that to the old stories of
the Indians, from the pioneer times. An Indian throws
himself on the ground and he listens, and he says that
two riders come there, two men on horses. He hears from
the ground. So, comparatively speaking, the analyst knows
what will come later on.

DR. FREEMAN: He doesn't know what it looks like, but
there is something coming, or a special kind of . . .

DR. REIK: Yes.

DR. FREEMAN: The issue in this case was that it was unorthodox. I happened to have time—it was my vacation.
Now this patient would start to talk and things would
come pouring out, and I had the sense that I had someone
on the precipice—just a step beyond and he would fall
over, and I had the chance to get him just before he fell.
First, to maintain his stability, and then to pull him back.

DR. REIK: You were on vacation at the time?

DR. FREEMAN: I was in New York on my vacation,
which meant I had lots of time. But sometimes a single
session would last three hours, simply because I felt at no
point could I cut him off. He would go through crisis
after crisis, but then they passed. It was as though there
is a large boil which has to be lanced before it explodes and
kills him.

DR. REIK: Yes, an emergency situation.

DR. FREEMAN: The interesting thing was that this was

a patient who had lost all sense of himself—he couldn't criticize anybody, he felt he was a worm, he was nothing. Towards the termination, as it were, the time when he would have to go to work abroad, he sat up and he said: "I won't keep coming to you because you have a hell of a nerve! What do you mean, keeping me here three hours at a time?" And this was the one time I didn't keep him. But he said: "How dare you! I told my friends that some of these sessions last two hours, sometimes three hours, and they said that's unethical." And I thought it was great, because he could assert himself about something and even criticize an authority figure.

DR. REIK: In an extraordinary situation, you need extraordinary measures.

DR. FREEMAN: As long as the relationship remains analytic, all the necessary procedures are appropriate?

DR. REIK: Yes, it would seem so.

✳

DR. REIK: There is something about the patient-therapist interaction which is unknown to an outsider and that is beyond the reach of reason. Perhaps that can be illustrated with the following incident.

A colleague was reporting on a case and as he described the patient I began using the technique of "Listening with the Third Ear." It was as if I were listening to the patient herself and my own thoughts were making associations with what was being said.

I remembered Freud telling us of the dream of a woman who was always a passionate horserider, and then I had a memory of a patient I had forty years ago in Vienna. She was a physician and she was also an avid rider, but she rode horses mostly when she was menstruating. That was at a time when there was no such thing as Tampax or such.

I always thought it must be damned uncomfortable. But she was a physician so she must have known what she was doing. That was the first association.

As I continued listening to the analyst reporting his case, I had a second association. During the First World War, I served in the Austrian Army as a second lieutenant and toward the end of the war, I was sent back to Vienna for two weeks because I was ill. My task was to train cavalry reservists. We had a surgeon who was also training cavalry, and I heard him say one day to the reservists: "God have mercy on your wives if you can't ride them better than this mare." That was the second idea. It didn't make any sense to me.

Then the word "Penthesilea" came into my mind. Penthesilea was queen of the Amazons, a mythical tribe of women who rode horseback. In order to fight better, they cut off their right breasts. The Amazons were always fighting the Greeks, and Penthesilea herself was killed by Achilles at Troy. Then I remembered the famous German writer, Heinrich von Kleist, who was emotionally disturbed and who wrote a play called "Penthesilea." In the play, Penthesilea was very beautiful and when Achilles killed her he was very sad. That was the last association.

During the discussion of the case the analyst had reported on, I said that his woman patient showed a tendency to disavow part of her feminity and instead of the desire to be ridden, she rides. It is a reversal, and she is always in conflict with men. That diagnosis was later confirmed. How did my own associations connect? First was the woman physician who was riding only when she was menstruating. Second was the surgeon who said to the reservists: "God have mercy on your wives if you can't ride them better than this mare." Third was Penthesilea and the Amazons. So you see how I came to that conclusion? The thoughts seemed to interfere, but as a matter of fact they helped. They are like elves that do the helping in the night.

DR. FREEMAN: It is as though the unconscious were the same for everyone, so that if you can dip into your own, you are in contact with the patient's.

DR. REIK: Very good. That means that nothing that is human is alien to me. Men or women.

DR. FREEMAN: A sensitive analyst automatically does what he asks the patient to do. The patient describes a feeling, and we say to the patient—of course I'm simplifying this—"There was another time when you felt this way. And we will retrace it." I think that is what you were doing when you heard the material—there was another time you reacted this way and you traced it.

DR. REIK: That's a good explanation, and it worked that way even with memories of Vienna forty years ago.

Well, now I give you a case of another analyst. There was a woman who was a substitute teacher and who for a long time postponed her exam. The peculiarity of this patient was that she could not express emotion in words. She could only act. She came from Poland, and when she was a little girl her father was taken by the Nazis. She thought her father was taken away because she was naughty. And she waited, believing that if she will be nice her father will be returned to her.

Also, she had terrible fights with her mother. Her mother was very severe and she shouted at her mother, "Drop dead." So her analyst told her this was a death wish. And the patient denied that. "It is not a death wish, it is only what I said." The analyst came from Munich and she remembered two men had a fight and one of them said: "*Leck mich im Arsch.*" The other man sued him, and the judge freed the first man, because, the judge said: "In Munich that is only an idiomatic way of expressing something else." Now let's go back to this patient.

She was entirely unable to keep discipline in her class. Once during class a little girl took out a doll and caressed it. And the patient, without a word, took the doll from the little girl and threw it out of the window. She could not verbally express emotion. Now, more of the story of this patient. When she was twenty-one, in college, she got into an affair with a professor. He was married and had three children and would not divorce. She got pregnant and as she lived with her mother, the whole thing was impossible. She had an abortion. So her behavior as a teacher meant that she did to the little girl the same thing that happened to herself. In addition, she also acted out the part of her own mother. I asked the analyst: "Did the patient tell the story of the abortion? Did you go into that?" And the therapist said, "No." And I said: "You have to make her go into it and relive it again and again. Because a first abortion is a traumatic event for a girl." She followed my advice, with the effect that the girl became interested in what happened with the doll, and thought about what it would be like if she had had the child. It would have been nine years old now, and so on. She lived through her feelings about this, which she had always before pushed aside. It was the beginning of her recovery.

DR. FREEMAN: What about a patient's conscious or unconscious diagnosis of himself?

DR. REIK: Sometimes they say something. One woman patient had no idea about herself at first. So she said: "What do you think is the matter with me?" And I said to her: "I think you have a paranoic trait." And she said: "I heard that before somewhere. My father was declared paranoic." But one could say that some people have some sensitivity to their basic problems. However, they don't quite understand what they are saying. And then they forget it. They may say: "I have an obsession," or "an anxiety," or such, which in most cases is correct. One patient said: "People go through my things and take away my bras." She neglected to say whether it is men or women who took her things. She believes her sister-in-law says derogatory things about her on the telephone and talks about her, like the actors say, in an aside. Then she says: "I want my child to go to private school and my ex-husband says she should go to public school, and he hit me." Now, I don't know whether that is true, or whether this is only in her imagination.

DR. FREEMAN: Why did she leave her husband?

DR. REIK: He was an artist and he was psychotic. She had gotten into an affair with him and couldn't get out of it anymore, so she married him, you know? The interesting thing is that in sexual intercourse she functions very well.

DR. FREEMAN: It stands to reason. Because if she is escaping homosexuality, she would see to it that heterosexual activity would not be disturbed.

DR. REIK: Yes, she fights off homosexuality. She says, for instance, that among the most derogatory things which her sister-in-law says about her is that she, the patient, has amorous designs on her.

DR. FREEMAN: Is paranoia generally an unconscious fight against homosexuality?

DR. REIK: In general, yes. That is in two forms. In the form of projection or in the form of persecution. I give you an instance. We lived in another apartment and a patient went to the window and said: "Look at that man on the street there, do you see that other one over there also? They all want to make me." That would be projection. Because he projects his own homosexual wishes onto them. The paranoid form, the persecution form, would be that a man would say: "Look at these two men there in the street, they are my enemies. They want to send electric rays through my body, and kill me." It is the same as before, but a different form of the fantasy. It amounts to a negation of homosexuality and turning it into hostility.

DR. FREEMAN: But the origin is the same, the dynamic is the same?

DR. REIK: Yes, the refusal or rejection of homosexuality.

DR. FREEMAN: I thought we might talk about interpretation of dreams.

DR. REIK: In dream interpretation, you have to use the associations of the patient all the time. But certain things the patient doesn't know. Two of those are always there. One is the symbolism in dreams. The symbolism is, so to speak, an *Urgut*, an ancestral inheritance of mankind, which the patient doesn't know. For instance, that a car is a woman's body, umbrella is a penis, or such things. That is one thing. But the other is, of course, the resistance, or the transference in general, positive to negative. Freud had a patient who once met his daughter, Anna, on the staircase and later he told Freud about a dream. "In the dream," he said, "I met a girl going down your stairway, and the girl had two big pieces of shit instead of eyes." Freud interpreted that very clearly. That means she has much money. Feces is money, that's always the symbolism. The patient thought: "She has plenty of money," because of her father, of course. So, the patient thought: "Eventually I could marry that girl because she had plenty of money." That came out from the associations later on.

DR. FREEMAN: One of my patients had an interesting dream. He dreamed that as he was walking someone came at him and threw a knife; the knife cut his finger and it stuck. He pulled the knife out and said: "That's not so bad. It's going to stop bleeding and I have to go and do something anyway." End of the dream.

DR. REIK: No association?

DR. FREEMAN: None. He said he was surprised when he got hit. I asked him how he felt when he woke up and he said a little irritated because he had wanted to see what was going to happen next.

DR. REIK: Could that not be a castration wish? Wish, not fear. It need not be a fear. Every man sometimes thinks about what it would be like if he were a woman? That is like a fantasy—in the category of: "What it would be like if I were president of the United States." That is a harmless wish.

The extent to which dreams reflect unconscious material varies a great deal. Sometimes the material seems not pre-conscious or subconscious, but semi-conscious, as though the patient were partly aware of what the meaning was. When the dream resembles a fantasy, it is almost as though it were not unconscious.

There is a difference between unconscious and repressed. Unconscious is something which is not quite there but which can be recalled anytime with some help. But re-pressed means that there is a hindrance against something becoming conscious. I give you an instance of that. Last week I saw a patient who had been with me a few years ago. He came back only for a consultation on account of a marital conflict. And I remember during the whole time of his analysis he had one thing against me. Whenever I would rub my face, he would insist that I'm yawning—that I'm bored with him. I didn't deny anything. When he came back, he said: "Now you made the same movement which you did in my analysis." He insisted that I was always bored with him. It was a negative transference.

DR. FREEMAN: Were you bored with him?

DR. REIK: No, not at all. And certainly not at the moment when I made that gesture.

But apropos of dreams, I remember the following one

a patient had. A man, near forty, who dreamed that there is a party in his house. The party is not planned, but is, so to speak, a kind of surprise party. There are many people there and he comes there in the moment when his wife and his mother come out of the bathroom. And his mother is only half-dressed, half-naked, and he's very angry, not about that, but he says to his mother: "What are you doing there? Why are you here?"

In order to interpret the dream, it is necessary to know the situation of the man. The man is married and has a child. Since the child was born, he is impotent. The child is now five years old. The wife is one year older than he is. They have separate bedrooms and he usually sleeps badly. The night of the dream his father-in-law was visiting them, so he had to share the same bedroom with his wife. Before he went to the bedroom, he saw his wife sitting and reading, and her skirt was very high up, which made him desire her for a moment. But only for a moment. It was his mother's birthday and his wife gave his mother a present, stockings or so. This man sees in his wife, who is a year older, kind of a mother figure. So, in the dream he had thought: "Let's have a party." In American slang "Let's have a party" could mean a proposition—a sexual proposition. So while there is a party going on which is not planned but a surprise, it leads back to this one moment of desire when he saw his wife.

And the second thing is that his little son was out of the room when she was reading. So the dream means: "I want to have a party and I want it to be a surprise," because he had not approached his wife. Well, she reminds him of his mother whom he sees there half-dressed, and he is angry that she reminds him of his mother.

DR. FREEMAN: Would you say there is a psychological

difference in a man's relationship to his father and a woman's relationship to her mother?

DR. REIK: There is a difference between men and women, between little boys and little girls.

I would say it is psychologically necessary that a boy measures himself against his father and thinks he should surpass his father, socially, in his accomplishments, and in all other directions. It is necessary for the man. The culture in which a son does exactly the same as the father doesn't progress, it gets fossilized—like the old Jewish Orthodox culture, or the old Chinese culture for centuries remained the same, without progress. But in the cultures in which a son wants to surpass his father there is progress.

Now, we see the contrast to the little girl. The little girl does not want to surpass her father, but wants to replace her mother—only to replace. I remember that my little daughter said: "When mother goes away, I will cook for you." She was then five years old. That means she takes the place of mother, not surpass. Although later on perhaps that comes too, that she will be a better wife or cook for her husband.

DR. FREEMAN: Why doesn't she want to surpass her?

DR. REIK: Because the drives, the aggressive drives, the apparent drives are not so great as in the little boy.

DR. FREEMAN: So, the little boy doesn't want to replace his father, he wants to best him.

DR. REIK: Yes. To go *beyond* him.

DR. FREEMAN: What about the women who want to go beyond their mothers, does that mean that they have a stronger aggressive drive?

DR. REIK: I would say they have more ambition, if it is not in the field of women.

DR. FREEMAN: What about the intervention of the analyst in a reality situation—the personal morality of the analyst. How does it enter into a situation when it comes to suicide or abortion, for instance? Suppose a patient came to you and said she needed an abortion. I happen to think it should be legal, but I can't say that to a patient. What would you do?

Dr. Reik: I would leave it to the patient. But look, there are a few psychoanalytic principles which are involved. The first is that you never tell the patient what he should do, but only what he should not do. That means you protect the patient from self-damage, from self-inflicted pain. So I would say the following: The decision has to be made by the patient whether she wants to have the child or not. Then, if she wants to have an abortion, you help. For instance, I have sent patients to psychiatrists to get certifications, because there are two psychiatrists necessary to certify if abortion is necessary.

Dr. Freeman: This is what I did with a patient's friend. My patient came and said: "My friend is from a very Orthodox Jewish family, and she's having a child by a man who doesn't love her, and she doesn't love him. I think if my friend goes home and tells her parents, her father will have a heart attack and die, because he has a very weak heart." I asked: "How does your friend feel about it?" My patient was very agitated. "Does she feel about it the way you do?" And she said: "No, my friend is very calm. When I asked her, 'What's going to happen?' she said, 'Nothing's going to happen, I'm going to kill myself.'" And the way my patient quoted her friend and imitated her as being so calm, so detached, it seemed obvious to me that her friend really meant to commit suicide. She wasn't being hysterical, she wasn't nervous or anything. So I gave my patient the name of a psychiatrist. But in a case where you know the patient is not likely to kill herself. . . .

DR. REIK: In that case also if the patient has made her decision to get an abortion, you would help her get the name of a psychiatrist. But you don't tell the patient what she should do, you should be like the Ten Commandments. You always say *do not. Not do—but do not.*

I had a patient, a writer who was offered the position of editor of a literary magazine, and he talked to me of what a terrible thing it was to make a decision. Should he stay with his magazine where he is a critic, or should he take over the other thing? For the other thing there is more money and more reputation and so on. On the other hand, he does not know if he is good enough, whether he could do all these things, whether he could fulfill all the requirements which these people want from him. And I told him that he has made his decision long ago, unconsciously. His behavior is as if a woman gets a proposal and stands before the mirror naked and says: "Will he be satisfied with me? My hips, my breasts?" I compare the situation with that of a Jewish girl . . . there is a Jewish proverb in which the girl plays coy, you know, with the man. The Eastern Jews say, "*Shlepp mich, ich geh gern*". . . . "Pull me, I'd just love to go." Excellent.

DR. FREEMAN: What happens if a patient senses disapproval in the analyst?

DR. REIK: Give me a "for instance."

DR. FREEMAN: Well, and this goes back to the topic of the value system of the analyst, I had a female homosexual patient. The mother was sick and the father over-aggressive. She had been an acting-out homosexual but had stopped. Then she met a girl who had no previous homosexual experience at all. The girl came from an upper middle class family, professional parents, and she had led a very sheltered and, up to that point, normal life. She represented to my patient the complete antithesis of herself. Her ideal. The girl was very shy, and not part of any group.

The patient made friends with her and proceeded to seduce her. The patient was sitting up when she told me this, and I tried to show no reaction, but there must have been something in my facial expression that indicated disapproval.

DR. REIK: How old is the girl?

DR. FREEMAN: They were both sixteen. And she said: "You don't approve of my doing that, do you?"

DR. REIK: You should have answered the opposite.

DR. FREEMAN: What worried me was that she would do it out of spite next time, because she felt I disapproved.

DR. REIK: But she did it already.

DR. FREEMAN: Yes, but she stopped with this one, after about two weeks. She said: "The girl is in love with me, I can't stand it, I don't want her near me. I can't have her around." She literally grew tired of her and was always very irritated with her.

DR. REIK: She had been testing her power to seduce her. It was not the attraction of the girl.

DR. FREEMAN: And each time she had someone she was go'ng to seduce, she would say: "You don't approve, do you?"

DR. REIK: I would shift the whole question. I would say: "It is as if a girl flirts with a man, seduces a man, not because she is attracted to him or because she wants him, but only to test her power of 'what can I do.' So you must have some doubts about your power, your attractiveness." That is how I would shift it. To the ego.

DR. REIK: Freud once said that we have lived under the illusion that people are more peaceable than they are. They have illusions also about sexual morality and about monogamy. You will admit that, biologically at least, women are much more inclined to stay with one man. And men the other way around.

DR. FREEMAN: I'm beginning to think that the sexual drive in men is not what it is cracked up to be. Not as profound. Not as insistent. Not as continual.

DR. REIK: No, don't say that. It is very urgent.

DR. FREEMAN: Urgent, but not necessarily frequent or continual, as our literature would have us believe. When it arises it is urgent.

DR. REIK: I like that pun. When it arises.

But Freud spoke of conditions of love, the division between sexuality and affection. I remember reading the sentence of Flaubert: *"Un jeune homme peut adorer une jeune femme et courir chez les filles chaque soir."* A young man can adore a certain woman and run every evening to the prostitutes.

For a man, seduction doesn't mean a damn thing. It is just a roll in the hay.

DR. FREEMAN: But it must mean something to them. Why else do they keep talking about it and feel guilty?

DR. REIK: Towards father. Not on account of sex itself. The thought: "If father knew what I'm doing he would scold me." The Oedipus situation is behind that guilt.

DR. FREEMAN: In other other words the guilt that a man feels when he commits adultery . . .

DR. REIK: If there is such a guilt . . .

DR. FREEMAN: Well, then the guilt that he professes to feel.

DR. REIK: It might also be connected with quite different things. For instance, with a thought like: "I wish my wife would die, then I would have many other girls." It need not always be connected with the father. But guilt feeling is always, without exception, connected with violent or murderous wishes. Never with sex, never with sex directly. Even a boy who masturbates and feels guilty afterwards has left out something. Namely the thought: "If my mother or father would come in now and disturb me or reproach me, I would feel so mad I would kill them." The guilt feeling concerns this intermediary thought of murder. Never, never with sex. You can always trace it back, with all your patients, to violent tendencies and impulses.

Dr. Freeman: What about the possibility that a man's promiscuity or availability to every woman is a kind of fear of homosexuality, or escape from it?

Dr. Reik: Yes, certainly. Otto Rank said that behind that is really a deep flight from homosexuality. That is one interpretation. The other possibility, of course, would be to look at the thing as: "All these women cannot substitute for the one woman—the mother."

Dr. Freeman: Is the answer to this, for some men, marrying an older woman?

Dr. Reik: Sometimes, yes. Which need not be bad at all. Think of Disraeli, about whom Maurois wrote one of the biographies. Disraeli's wife was sixteen years older than he.

Dr. Freeman: In other words, if a young man falls in love with an older woman and marries her, it is not necessarily pathological?

Dr. Reik: No, not necessarily. I wouldn't say so.

Dr. Freeman: Well, what are some of the reasons that this might happen?

Dr. Reik: Well, in the case of Disraeli, he was a young, promising politician. She was an older woman, and an aristocrat. It was a search for his mother, but not damaging. And, of course, she brought him out.

Dr. Freeman: Are there any other reasons?

Dr. Reik: There might be. The dignity of the woman, which might be in some cases more than the man.

Dr. Freeman: Then a young man falling in love with an

older woman, or vice versa, does not necessarily imply pathology?

DR. REIK: No, I wouldn't say so.

DR. FREEMAN: So the dynamics could be that (a) he's looking for his mother.

DR. REIK: Yes.

DR. FREEMAN: And (b) he's escaping from homosexuality—but that could be almost any marriage?

DR. REIK: No . . . any marriage?

DR. FREEMAN: I mean for such a man. It would not have to be an older woman.

DR. REIK: Yes. But perhaps it should be. Of course, Don Giovanni, he, so to speak, substitutes a whole sequence of women for the man. He runs away from homosexuality to many women.

DR. FREEMAN: One of my former patients considers himself a great lover. But I get the feeling that he's rather hostile towards women. He was having very negative feelings towards me which he couldn't express at all. All he did was keep dropping matches on the floor. He'd put them out, but they weren't out, or his cigarette would fall out of the ashtray still lit. So when I asked him what did he want to set on fire, he got very angry.

DR. REIK: The fire was meant for you. The subject got him angry.

DR. FREEMAN: Yes. So then I decided I'd better not pursue this, because he had not been in analysis long enough and he might be too frightened by it. Then I asked how he would feel about the possibility that he didn't like women in general. He became appalled by the idea. He said: "I don't see how you can say that because I think women are sweet and kind and lovable and adorable." And he stalked out. The next day he came back. "You know," he said, "I feel just great. When you said is it possible that maybe I didn't like women, I suddenly felt very mature, because all day long I went around saying, 'Gee, maybe I don't really like women, and isn't that grown up of me to be able not to like women?' " And then came the next association. He said: "Then I thought to myself that all these girls I sleep with, whenever I have intercourse with them, I say to myself, 'All right. Take this! And this! I'll get you.' Each time."

What if you have a young patient who is not afraid of homosexuality. But homosexuality is the real problem, even though the presenting symptoms have nothing to do with it.

DR. REIK: If he functions normally sexually, then don't discuss it. Leave it alone. Everybody has a certain homosexuality. In everybody's dreams homosexuality appears. If there would be one day after the other, one dream after the other for a long time, for many months, then you would discuss it.

DR. FREEMAN: If eventually he says that he has a compulsive fear of homosexuality, how do you handle it?

DR. REIK: You cannot deny it.

DR. FREEMAN: The only way to save him from the complete breakdown would be to help him cope with the fact that he was . . .

DR. REIK: Anna Freud had such a case in which a man came and was treated for two reasons: he was homosexual and he had a very serious obsession. She came so far that she got rid of the obsession, but not the homosexuality. Don't forget, homosexuality can only be cured, so to speak, if there is a contradiction in the patient himself. Otherwise not.

DR. FREEMAN: Then the thing to have done in a case like this is to adjust him to his homosexuality, because this . . .

DR. REIK: Yes, if there is nothing else . . .

DR. FREEMAN: Because this was his morbid fear, that he

would be homosexual, and he was frightened of it, and this was what . . .

DR. REIK: Well, had he practiced homosexuality before?

DR. FREEMAN: He had been driven to it, apparently. He married as a defense against it. He was always sort of effeminate, he was always drawn to men, but he fought it for years.

DR. REIK: There are cases in which a person is effeminate without being homosexual. I explained that once to a patient. It's so as if we'd say: "I want to go to Canada and I come to Boston." Boston is on the way to Canada, but it is not Canada. For instance, I once saw a case: A boy was furiously jealous of his sister, because she was preferred. He thought: "They'd love me more if I were a girl." But he wasn't homosexual, he was feminine.

DR. FREEMAN: But one does not deny . . .

DR. REIK: No, no, I wouldn't deny it. But I would say: "Look here. What about your self-damaging things, masochistic habits?"

DR. FREEMAN: If a patient says he's driven by guilt about this particular thing, do you alleviate the guilt and become permissive, and say: "All right, if that's how you feel . . ."

DR. REIK: Nietzsche said: "To repent something is stupid." Nothing is accomplished by it, you know? After you have done something, it should be done with.

DR. FREEMAN: But supposing for the moment there is only a wish, the obsessive wish, guilt-ridden?

DR. REIK: A wish to what?

DR. FREEMAN: To become involved in homosexual activity.

DR. REIK: No, that is not so. Guilt is always connected with violence.

DR. FREEMAN: Then if someone is on the verge of having a homosexual affair . . . say they fall in love with someone and they want to have an affair. They don't really know what they want, but that could become part of the relationship.

DR. REIK: But the patient feels guilty about the idea of it, in other words, she feels that it's immoral. Good. Then you lead her back to childhood. If mother would know that, she would scold me and I would like to kill her.

DR. FREEMAN: This removes the guilt, but does this then free her to go about the affair?

DR. REIK: This is not your business what she does. She has to decide herself.

DR. FREEMAN: Assuming that in this patient there is a tremendous measure of anxiety about sexual relationships.

DR. REIK: Well, we analyze that. And she never had sexual intercourse?

DR. FREEMAN: Yes, she did, she is married.

DR. REIK: There are other reasons then.

❧

DR. FREEMAN: What about the supposed link between homosexuality and racial prejudice? Is that just a wild assumption?

DR. REIK: No, it's not, when you think that the carriers of racial prejudice are mostly men. Women are less inclined to this racial prejudice.

DR. FREEMAN: Women are *less* inclined?

DR. REIK: Yes. You do not think that?

DR. FREEMAN: I don't know. I was thinking of the school integration in the South—those women who stood around and jeered at the black children going to school. But I don't know if perhaps this is some other thing having to do with their own frustrations in other areas. Somehow those women seemed more masculine, or married spinsters a long time removed from the connubial bed.

DR. REIK: Yes, but in general, women are less prejudiced. Since we speak about that—the other day I took a bus and there was a Negro driver. Behind him sat a Negro woman with whom he talked. And he said to her: "Look, in twenty years the whole Negro question will be solved. Think of the Jewish question. More than three thousand years it took to be solved."

Dr. Freeman: When is a patient ready to end analysis?

Dr. Reik: There are some criteria for termination. I use always the same comparison. Let's say you have a little boy or little girl who has to go to school. You at first go up to the classroom door with the little boy or girl. Then you go only to the entrance of the school and the child goes in alone. Then you go only until across the street, then you go only till the corner, and finally the child goes alone to school. That stage has to be reached, of course. That means independence from the anayst.

Dr. Reik: I got a telephone call from a new group that formed, and they asked me to join them. They called themselves "Freudian Psychoanalysts." I said to them: "I didn't know that there was another kind of psycho-analyst." In our times, 1915 or so, they called us Freudians. There is a story about Schubert. When Schubert lived in Vienna, the musical life there was divided into two camps, the one were the Beethovians, and the other were the Mozartians. And they fought. And when Schubert was asked whether he considered himself a Beethovianer or Mozartianer, he said: "*Ich bin selber aner.*" I cannot translate that very well. It literally means "I'm one my-self."—He felt that he was himself.

A student recently asked me how many psychoanalytic movements there are today. I told him there are many. Freud said that there will come a time of *pénétration pacifique*, peaceful penetration of the teaching into a wide circle, and with that a dilution. There are very few psychoanalysts today who adhere to the concept of infantile sexuality. People have in fact repressed again or suppressed whatever tremendous strides that Freud made. And this is not out of ignorance. It seems a kind of inner psychological need. And it isn't only with patients. But Freud foresaw that there will be modification. He wasn't as dogmatic as they make him out. Most people, even analysts, are afraid, for example, of their unconscious incestuous fantasies. I had such fantasies about my two daughters. You have seen my two daughters—they are nice, no?

DR. REIK: One of my friends told the story of the analyst's nightmare. An analyst dreams that he is listening to a patient, and he wakes up and it is true.

FREUD

DR. FREEMAN: Did you see the play "The Far Country?"

DR. REIK: Yes.

DR. FREEMAN: Was it true to Freud?

DR. REIK: Yes, quite. There were some very realistic things. The scene in the play where Freud falls asleep at his desk late at night, exhausted, wakes in the morning and the first thing he does is take a cigar. He always had a cigar.

DR. FREEMAN: Did you like the way Freud was characterized?

DR. REIK: I would say it was too vivid. Freud had more self-control. He was a reserved man.

DR. FREEMAN: Was Freud's mother as tyrannical as she appeared?

DR. REIK: No, she was not a tyrant. But you can't expect a play to catch everything. For instance, in the play she calls Freud "My dear Sigmund," which she would never

79

have done. She always called him, "Siggy—*mein-Gold*."

DR. FREEMAN: My golden one?

DR. REIK: Yes. She did not speak in high German but Galician Yiddish.

DR. FREEMAN: What did you think of the portrayal of Freud's wife?

DR. REIK: Quite good but not quite accurate. She really never understood why her husband became famous. And she didn't understand his work; she was not particularly interested in his research. She had little awareness of the important role of the unconscious. Once she said to me about a hysterical woman we knew: "She'll get over it if she'll use her will." But she was a wonderful wife to Freud. For instance, she loved opera. But she never in her whole life got a chance to hear the overture in the Vienna opera house, because that was the time he had his dinner and she wanted to be there when he had his dinner. So she came always late, although she lived very near the Opera theater in the Berggasse. And I remember once when I visited him, it was raining, and when we went out she went after him and said: "Sigmund, your galoshes." We were downstairs already. She was an excellent housewife too, and even though later on they had plenty of money she never let the maid do the shopping. She wanted to go herself to the market.

When we were all in the Semmering in the summers, she often talked to me, and we used to take walks. She had a strange, dry kind of humor. She said, for instance: "I get along famously with my daughters-in-law. I never see them." Besides that, at this time she talked often about psychoanalysis, about which she had only a vague idea. She said for instance: "Oh, well, hysteria and so on. We had also our troubles when we were young. But comes the menopause, then it's over." But she said to me that she never understood what is so great about analysis. And

only late in Freud's life when the Vienna Post Office
at his seventieth birthday opened offices on a Sunday only
for him, for all the letters and telegrams he got, only then
something dawned on her of his importance.

DR. FREEMAN: To her it only mattered that he was her
husband?

DR. REIK: Yes.

DR. FREEMAN: How did he feel about this? About her
not sharing his work?

DR. REIK: I don't know. Freud talked about his work to
his sister-in-law, whom I knew quite well. He made some
trips with her. She was much younger than Mrs. Freud,
and there were suspicions that he had an affair with her.
Nothing of the kind, I don't believe it. Freud had a certain
puritanical trend in his nature.

DR. FREEMAN: Then one could almost say he had a
marriage like the ancient Greeks. Two wives, one for
his children and one for his mind . . .

DR. REIK: Yes.

DR. FREEMAN: Is it true that Freud was celibate at about
thirty-five?

DR. REIK: No. Forty-five. Early, early.

I think generally he was only a tolerable husband but an
excellent father.

DR. FREEMAN: His daughter never married?

DR. REIK: No. Anna was originally a teacher. Later she
founded child analysis. Anna did not like me especially,
I don't know why, but she never seemed to like me.

DR. FREEMAN: How did that manifest itself?

DR. REIK: Well, I must have teased her in Vienna. She
wore skirts down to here, and she didn't pay any attention
to her appearance. And I said to her: "Oh, you will
change and have nice dresses and shoes and stockings and
so on." And she said: "No, never," and she was right.

DR. FREEMAN: Did Freud ever have any feelings about her appearance?

DR. REIK: No, I don't think so. He saw her differently. That is how it is with one's children. I have two daughters. I never learned to drive a car, but I am never nervous when I am in a car. Except when they drive. Yet one of them is married, the other one has her Ph.D., and I say: "Be attentive," "Be careful," and so on, because unconsciously I see them as little girls. Consciously I know they are grown up, but unconsciously, of course, I see them as little girls.

At the time I knew Anna she was a teacher in public school, but she slowly made her transition to becoming a child analyst. She had excellent intuitive understanding and fine perceptiveness. I will give you an instance of her perceptiveness. I remember one of the first patients she had was the young son of one of our analysts in Vienna. This little boy had a very conspicuous symptom. When he walked he made two steps forward and one step back. He was about eight or nine years old. After she had analyzed him for several months, Anna said to the little boy: "You know, Michael, your parents don't love each other," which was true. The after-effect of this declaration was that the symptom stopped. I call that really perceptive. But, of course, this was months after the analysis had started and she must have felt the inkling of the whole process already, and the emotion. She worked with what is called the surprise technique, which came from Freud. Breakthrough. This is something for which the boy was not prepared at all. And it broke through like a cannonball shatters a fortification. And the symptom disappeared shortly thereafter. As a matter of fact his parents did divorce later.

Anna herself, you know, was analyzed by Lou Andrea Salome, whom Freud himself had analyzed. The Princess

Bonaparte and Lou Andrea were the only women in that circle of psychoanalysts. Lou Andrea I knew very well. She was a friend of Nietzsche. Think of that.

DR. FREEMAN: Do you think Nietzsche went crazy because of his love for Lou Andrea Salome?

DR. REIK: No, he had syphilis. Incidentally, so did Heine. I knew Lou Andrea at the time when she was a friend of Rainer Maria Rilke. Rilke, of course, was one of the great German lyric poets. Did you know that I knew him? We were in the army together. One day the *Feldwebel* made the roll call. And when he said "Rainer *Maria* Rilke," he asked, "Why not Mitzi?" You see he couldn't understand that Rilke was named after his mother.

DR. FREEMAN: What was Freud's relationship with his children?

DR. REIK: There was no strain with Freud and his daughter, but there was some with his sons. They always wanted money. He gave them money.

DR. FREEMAN: You said he was an excellent father but a tolerable husband.

DR. REIK: Tolerant too. For instance, he did not like music very much. About Wagner he said: "In Wagner there is an idealism which is typical of juveniles, adolescents." He liked only the *Siegfried Idyll* and the *Meistersinger*, nothing else. The others he couldn't stand.

DR. FREEMAN: I agree with him about Wagner. But didn't he like any kind of music? Not even Mozart?

DR. REIK: Not much. He was a *type visuel*. The French psychologists differentiate between a *type visuel* and a *type auditif*. That means some people who remember better what a person looks like, and some remember better what a person sounds like and what a person says. I was entirely "auditif," and Freud was entirely "visuel." I remember during the summers on the Semmering we sometimes went collecting mushrooms. I never saw them, but he always knew where they are—he saw them immediately. His glance was very sharp and observant, while mine was not. Perhaps that is why I wrote *Listening With The Third Ear*.

DR. FREEMAN: Didn't he like art, painters?

DR. REIK: No, sculpture mostly. Not many painters, except Rembrandt.

DR. FREEMAN: What did you think of Ernest Jones' biography of Freud?

DR. REIK: It is excellent in general. He made only two mistakes. One was about Freud's Jewishness, and the other was about Freud's relationship to Vienna. He thought Freud had nothing Jewish about him except his great love for Jewish stories, Jewish wit and jokes. Jones thought of Jews as primal Jews, Talmudists, and those who talk *pilpul*. You know what *pilpul* is?

DR. FREEMAN: Yes.

DR. REIK: A certain way of questioning and reasoning, shrewd and so on.

DR. FREEMAN: Like the joke: "Two Jews, three opinions."

DR. REIK: Sometimes even four. But Freud didn't have the traits of the primal Jew. Still, that is not the only part of being a Jew, and Jones did not understand that you can be Jewish deep in the pit of your personality without representing the "Jewish type."

DR. FREEMAN: In other words, since Freud didn't fit the stereotype of what a Jew was, Jones automatically considered him un-Jewish? A little unconscious anti-Semitism?

DR. REIK: Yes, a little. After all, every one has a little. He thought Freud had nothing that's Jewish, in spite of the attitude of Freud himself, who always said that he was proud of being a Jew.

The other thing Jones did not understand was the relationship of Freud to Vienna. All the time I knew him, Freud abused and cursed Vienna, made fun of the Viennese *Gemütlichkeit*. Yet he never went away from Vienna; he was bound to Vienna by a kind of hate-love. In the last twenty years of his life, Freud wanted to go to New York, to London, to Harvard, wherever, and he received many honorable offers, and most attractive financially. And yet he always refused. He remained since his childhood in Vienna, except for short trips to Italy and Holland. And he made one short trip to America. He didn't want to leave and renounce his claim. He hated Vienna and loved it at the same time. For instance, he made fun of the Viennese. He said: "In Vienna, if you take a cab and you ask the driver at the end, 'What do I owe you?' The driver would say, '*Was Sie Meinen.*'—'Whatever you think.' " It means the customer would pay much more than the driver knows he should get. And Freud compared that to the attitude of the Viennese to psychoanalysis, their sloppiness: "*Wer kann's nicht gebrauchen,*"—"Who can't use it," you know? As if it would be so it's not important. Also Freud sometimes imitated the Viennese dialect—he couldn't speak Viennese at all, but he imitated the dialect often. He made fun of it. But he could never leave Vienna.

DR. FREEMAN: Was this perhaps because he did not want to leave his mother?

DR. REIK: Perhaps. After she died, Freud sometimes said: "Now I can die." His desire to live was no longer so strong. I knew his mother when she was an old lady. She regularly went to Bad Ischl, near Salzburg, for the summers and I would see her there. She was made an honorary citizen because she went so many years.

DR. FREEMAN: How did Freud feel about women?

DR. REIK: He liked them. He was always very gallant to women. I was attending the International Psycho-

analytic Congress in March, 1914, with my wife. She was
still a bride, and she didn't know much about psychoanalysis. I introduced her to Freud, and she told him:
"There's really no place for me here." He said to her:
"You are the pearl of this Congress." In conversation with
me, he compared her to one of the madonnas of Botticelli.
Freud was in this direction very old-fashioned. He always
said: "The best woman is the one you don't talk about."
Neither praisingly nor derogatorily.

DR. FREEMAN: How did he mean that?

DR. REIK: It is an old German proverb. The best woman
is the one about whom we don't talk. The one about
whom no one talks. Well, it would not apply to many
women in his own circle, for instance the great Princess
Bonaparte or Lou Salome, who were psychoanalysts and
writers. Only later in life did Freud talk freer about his
relationship with women. He might have felt very much
attracted to some, but there was nothing else. He was a
highly moral man. But he was very stimulated by women,
especially by the Princess Bonaparte, a very, very beautiful
woman.

DR. FREEMAN: Very few people are aware of psychology
early in their lives. My husband says he didn't read Freud
till he was eleven.

DR. REIK: Yes, that's very amusing. But I didn't hear of
Freud until I was twenty-one. I was a student of psychology at the University of Vienna. We were interested in
sound threshold, perception—entirely physiological. Once
Professor Jodl was discussing the theories of Wundt and
Titchener, the famous psychologists at that time. Then he
said with a fine ironic smile: "There is a professor here in
Vienna who says that forgetting has not to do with association, but with repression." A few months later I read

The painting entitled "Spinoza Being Stoned by the Jews," which hung in Freud's office and testified to his own feelings about being ridiculed by his colleagues for his revolutionary theories.

Dr. Reik with Dr. Freeman at dinner in her home, New York, 1963. (PHOTO BY PAUL FREEMAN)

Dr. Reik in his office, New York, 1964. (PHOTO BY GERALD APPEL, M.S.S.)

Psychopathology of Everyday Life. It made a deep impression on me, and then I read everything Freud had written until then.

DR. FREEMAN: You had intended to go to medical school?

DR. REIK: Yes. My father died early, and we had at this time in Vienna a guardian, who had to tell me what to do. And this man wanted I should study law. And I fought him. Think if I had studied law. What should I do with Austrian law in America? It would have been terrible. I came here in 1938 when I was over fifty.

DR. FREEMAN: How did you first meet Freud?

DR. REIK: I had written my thesis on the psychology of the artist, about Flaubert and his book *La Tentation de Saint Antoine,* as I had studied French literature too. I got into a fight with my professors, because it was the first Ph.D. thesis exclusively using psychoanalytic methods. I sent the manuscript to Freud. He read it, and then he asked me to come to see him. I went to his home at 19 Berggasse. As I walked up the stairs, I felt like a young girl going on a date, my heart was beating so fast. Then I stood for the first time in the room where Freud worked, by his desk, surrounded by the Egyptian and Etruscan figurines he loved so much. He knew Flaubert's book much better than I, and we discussed it at length.

That year I was introduced as a guest at a meeting of the Vienna Psychoanalytic Society by Dr. Wilhelm Stekel. I did not only listen, but because I had read the psychoanalytic literature, felt I could take part in the discussion with here and there a remark.

After I had my Ph.D., I asked Freud if I should now study medicine. He said no, he had other plans for me. He urged me to give my life to psychoanalysis and psychoanalytic research. For two years then he gave me from his private pocket a certain amount monthly to study psychoanalysis. I was very poor. He also got me a job in

a bookstore in Vienna, so I could earn a little money.
The bookstore was run by Hugo Heller, who also arranged
concerts and lectures. I worked there preparing catalogues.
I remember in one of our brochures, we asked prominent
people their favorite books, and I remember still that
Freud said one of his favorites was Anatole France's *Sur
la Pierre Blanche.*

For two years Freud gave me a certain amount monthly.
He evidently believed in my talent for psychoanalytic
research. Especially after I wrote *The Puberty Rites of
Savages.* After my marriage, he appeared one day in our
shabby Berlin apartment, in January 1915. After walking
up four flights of stairs he brought the news that the
Psychoanalytic Society had decided to award me the prize
for the best scientific work in the field of applied psychoanalysis for that article. I can still see the smile on his
face as he told me. In the letters he wrote me in 1913
and which I published in *The Search Within*—of course,
most of the letters which I got were lost when I escaped
from the Nazis, but many were preserved—and in the
letters he sometimes accused me that I want to run away
from getting money from him. But he gave me money
even after I was married for a time.

DR. FREEMAN: That means you were one of his favorites
then?

DR. REIK: Not at first. At first it was Rank, no doubt
about it.

DR. FREEMAN: So it was after Rank broke with Freud
that you became his favorite.

DR. REIK: Yes, slowly. You know, I had two brothers,
Hugo and Otto. They were 15 and 17 years older than
I. And when I came as a guest, at first, in the Vienna
Psychoanalytic Society there were two lay-analysts there.
Namely, Hans Sachs and Otto Rank, who were con-
siderably older than I. Both my brothers were killed by

the Nazis, by the way, in Vienna. The one was killed, the other committed suicide.

DR. FREEMAN: And you did not have training-analysis with Freud?

DR. REIK: No, because he did not at this time take any of his students for training analysis. Instead, he wrote Dr. Karl Abraham in Berlin, who offered to take me into training-analysis for nothing. So I moved to Berlin with my wife and went to Dr. Abraham until I was called into the Austrian Army in 1915. My father was born in Hungary, so I had to go into a Hungarian regiment, a cavalry regiment. After the Great War, I returned to Vienna to practice psychoanalysis.

DR. REIK: It is quite interesting that when I was on the Semmering many people visited Freud there. For instance, Sinclair Lewis, the American writer, who at this time came with Dorothy Thompson. He was not married with her yet, he had a love affair with her. We spent an evening together, Freud and Sinclair Lewis and Dorothy Thompson and I, which was quite amusing. Sinclair Lewis was very witty. At this time he was writing *Elmer Gantry*.

DR. FREEMAN: What did Freud think of Sinclair Lewis?

DR. REIK: He was amused by him. I don't think he had read his novels. He read a lot, but he didn't read so much of American writers. He preferred Poe and especially Mark Twain. On the Semmering I went with him to one of the movies of Charlie Chaplin. He loved Charlie Chaplin.

I'll tell you a story. I treated a woman whose husband was an American representative to the League of Nations. And we went together with Freud to Semmering. She had a number of children. One boy got infantile paralysis and was seriously ill. Freud said that I should go to the airfield when the husband came from Geneva and give

him the news. I should go to the airfield, not the wife,
because they were not getting along well. The boy died
and then the man and his wife came together again. Their
marital conflict was patched up by the tragedy of their
common loss. And Freud said: "The ways of the Lord
are mysterious, but rarely pleasant."

In Vienna I saw with Freud, Romain Rolland, Thomas
Mann, Tagore, Schnitzler, whose correspondence with
Freud is now published, and Stefan Zweig. A few other
writers too. To my astonishment, Freud liked Arnold
Zweig very much. Arnold not Stefan. They were not
related. Freud remembered Zweig's first novel, *Claudia.*
He had thought that it must have been a woman who
wrote it, because it showed such an intuitive understanding
of what women feel. Only later he heard that it is Arnold
Zweig. Zweig later lived in the Russian zone of Germany,
then he went to Palestine as it was then called. And when
I went to Palestine to visit my son, Zweig, who lived in
Haifa, heard that I was there and asked me to visit him.
He lived on Mount Carmel. He had a very nice house.
We spent a very nice evening there on Mount Carmel
with that wonderful view of the harbor of Haifa.

DR. FREEMAN: Was it true that Freud considered Arthur
Schnitzler his *Doppelgänger?*

DR. REIK: Yes. They met rather late in life. And another person whom Freud met very late was Beer Hoffman.
Beer Hoffman came to him when the Nazis were already
in Vienna. Hoffman died here in America, by the way.

On one of the walks I took with Freud in the garden,
he said that Hitler would never come to Austria because
the Allies would not allow that. But Hitler did come to
Vienna. Freud was not very good in the direction of
politics. For instance, he said: "One asks oneself, a bit
worried, what will the Bolsheviks have left to do when

they have exterminated all the bourgeois? What remains there for them to do?" When Freud heard that the Nazis, who were not yet in Vienna, had burned his books he said: "It's remarkable how the progress of civilization works. A few centuries ago they would have burned the person himself and not his books." As a matter of fact, that was too hasty a statement, because as you know, the crematoria later on, and the gas chambers, showed that that was continued. In general I would say that Freud was a bad prophet with regard to history and politics.

You know, when the Nazis came to Vienna, they ordered Freud to come to a certain office. Anna said to them: "My father is eighty-one years old, he doesn't go out anymore." So they went to his place and took all the money they found, of course, and ordered what they called "house arrest." The Princess Bonaparte was responsible for getting him out to England, by paying the Nazis the ransom they demanded for Freud. She really was a wonderful human being and a good friend.

Dr. Freeman: What form did Freud's teaching take?

Dr. Reik: It was quite a different way of teaching in those days. We were together in seminar, which was every day. Also he gave lectures which were not restricted to psychiatrists, in the psychiatric department at the university. There were psychologists and writers and other people there. And there were seminars of the Vienna Psychoanalytic Society, whose secretary I was after Otto Rank left. The general idea was that Freud was there at the seminars mostly because one of us gave a lecture or a conference and then there was discussion (Nunberg published some of the minutes). In general, Freud spoke at the end, after he had heard all others speak. I remember someone once described a program of what analysis could or should do in all fields, but this speaker remained very superficial. I sat at Freud's left side, and he gave me a little paper on which he had written: "Are you satisfied just reading the menu?" You know, because the speaker was so general, so superficial.

DR. FREEMAN: How long did Freud feel that the training analysis should last?

DR. REIK: He had no expressed views about it. But he thought a long time in general. One of the early analysts who came to Vienna complained about the training analysis, that Freud almost never spoke, only in the later part of her analysis.

DR. FREEMAN: Did he feel there were some people who were not suitable to be analysts?

DR. REIK: Yes, he thought that. But on the other hand he took a lot of people, because the first students were all not analyzed. Only the later ones were analyzed by Freud. But later still he stopped analyzing his students, because some of them broke from him and that gave him pain. And so, me, for instance, he sent to Karl Abraham in Berlin for analysis. Many years later, however, he did also analyze me during a crisis time.

DR. FREEMAN: You said that Freud thought that in the early days when the Americans came they were about the worst material to train as analysts?

DR. REIK: Yes. That means that he got Americans who had no time, for whom the running after the dollar was so important that they were not willing to stay a longer time.

You know when Dorothy Burlingham—she was the daughter of Tiffany—came back from studying in Vienna her sister waited for her at the harbor in New York. "Tell me, what did you learn in Vienna? What did it all amount to?" And she said that it was something very astonishing to her. "The main thing in life is feeling." The Americans were quite unaware of that in those days. Rational, nothing else. So that was very astonishing to her, that the main thing in life is feeling. That must have been in the beginning of the twenties. Except for a few like her, we got the worst people of America at that time, after the First World War. They stopped their training in analysis after six months or so. There was a psychiatrist who excused herself, she couldn't come for a session, for training. That means for training analysis. Imagine! She said she had to attend a course in the Vienna clinic. And Freud said: "Either analysis is the center of your life or you shouldn't come." So she gave up those other courses. There is something true in that. If you are in analysis, then analysis at a certain time should be the center of one's life. Everything else should be secondary for a while. Did I tell you that Freud thought that it was an American trait that they all mumble?

At a certain time he was bitter against the American analysts, just bitter. And he said that he regrets Columbus had discovered it. In 1910 he was already suspicious of America. He went with Ferenczi to the Niagara Falls. And he overheard two men speaking about him. One said: "That old chap there." Freud was fifty-six then. He didn't like this contempt for old age, this deification of youth. But this is a young country, relatively speaking.

Of course, it was a long time ago, but Freud said: "American mentality is characterized by 'unthinking optimism and empty activity.'" Unthinking optimism is correct. Absolutely correct. I remember when the United States went into the Second World War, I wanted to go to the army. I was fifty. The man there looked at me, surprised, and said: "What? The Germans kill people? Jews or others? Nonsense." And that is how that American

talked. The other part is, of course, also true. The empty
activity. Think of the Kinsey report. What is there?

✻

DR. FREEMAN: How would you describe Freud's analytic technique?

DR. REIK: Well, I can describe it perhaps by an instance.
After I was fifty, I returned for a short time to Freud
for what you would call after-analysis. My wife was at
this time very seriously ill and she died a short time afterwards. I suffered very much at this time. I went to Freud
for analysis, and as I lay there on the couch I played with
a small coin in my pocket and I said some stupid things,
I think about anal-erotic things. And Freud said: "No.
That is not right. I remind you that a minute before you
spoke of your brother. You said that when you were a
young analyst and went to Berlin to Dr. Abraham to go
into training-analysis, your brother at the station in Vienna
put a hundred marks into your pocket, which you found
later when you were on the train. And now that you
have a good practice, you are proud that you can send
money to your brother, who is retired and has little
money." That surprised me very much, but it was absolutely true.

DR. FREEMAN: In other words, he interpreted to the
patient what the patient was really saying?

DR. REIK: Yes. At the same time he listens to himself.
He listens to what comes out in himself. Therefore, we
are enemies of writing things down during the analytic
hour. When you are, so to speak, a magician, you cannot
afford to have a bad memory. Quite apart from the fact
that your attention is, of course, divided when you write
during the session.

Also Freud was not as orthodox in his technique as
people think. For instance, when he was in America, he did

not want to see any patients and referred neurotic patients to A. A. Brill and other psychoanalysts. Many patients and their relatives pleaded with Freud to treat them, but in vain. The husband of a woman who suffered from agoraphobia was especially insistent, and waited many hours to ask Freud again and again to see his wife. As we know, women with agoraphobia have unconscious temptation fantasies and protect themselves from this danger by crossing places and streets only in the company of a relative or friend. Finally this man pleaded with Freud to give him only a little piece of advice that would help to free his wife from the intensive anxiety when she is alone on a street. And Freud said, "Let her go out only when she wears dirty underwear."

DR. FREEMAN: Did Freud sometimes get angry at his patients?

DR. REIK: Only very rarely. Baron Dirstein, this masochistic patient who was with me, was with Freud before he came to me. Dirstein told me the following scene about Freud. He saw Freud deeply involved emotionally only once. At the end of an analytic session Dirstein got up from the couch and went to the door, and turning around to Freud, he said: "Do you think it would be good for me to go to Adler?" This was shortly after Freud's break with Adler. Freud didn't answer him. But Dirstein looked at him, and he saw that Freud's teeth were biting into the cigar in his mouth. That was an indication of how angry he was.

DR. FREEMAN: But he never expressed it?

DR. REIK: He never expressed it.

I remember a scene in which I was together with Pastor Pfister, who was one of the first students of Freud in Switzerland who applied analysis in his pastoral circle. And we were sitting there in the waiting room together, Pfister and I. Freud was in his room in consultation with

Professor Aschaffenburg, whom he quoted, by the way, in the *Psychopathology of Everyday Life*, but who was a terrible bore. Freud couldn't get rid of the man, he was too polite to get rid of him. So he stepped out of his office for a moment, and he said to Pfister: "Is it true that Christianity still forbids to kill people, at least in thoughts?" Then he stepped back into his office.

And once I was there when he was with the Baron Kaiserling, who wrote *Tagebuch eines Philosphen*, I think. Kaiserling talked a lot about analysis, and Freud said at a certain point to him: "*Sie verstehen ja das nicht.*" "You don't understand that."

One of the most interesting patients which Freud sent to me was Lord Namier, who is now dead. Namier was the son of a Polish Jew, and no one knew it at this time. He was then a lecturer—I think in Oxford or in Cambridge, I don't remember which—and was the expert on all Eastern European affairs. He was also secretary to Lord Cecil who was the British representative to the League of Nations. So Namier oscillated between the Foreign offices in London and Geneva and Vienna. So when he first came to me, I decided I cannot treat him because he was always away from Vienna several weeks, then he came back, and then went again away. But Freud persuaded me to take him. He called that Fractured Analysis. He was flexible in his technique. For instance, he analyzed Gustav Mahler for one whole afternoon. Mahler got some neurotic symptoms, and Bruno Walter persuaded him to go to Holland because Freud at this time was spending his vacation there.

I remember that Freud told me once of this analysis that Mahler had a *Marienkomplex*, a Holy Virgin complex, and that he saw his wife, Alma Maria, as kind of a holy virgin. Freud reproached him: "How can you treat a woman in this way who is so much younger than you?"

Also, Mahler was engrossed in his compositions, and also as director of the Vienna opera or the Philharmonic, and he often left her alone.

Apropos of Bruno Walter, he went to Freud because he always had a pain in the right arm, especially when he had to conduct. Freud asked Walter: "Have you ever been to Taormina?" Walter answered that he had not. "Take your wife there for one month," Freud said, "and I guarantee that after one year you will no longer have that pain." Walter took Freud's advice and went to Taormina. And indeed that pain did disappear after the year. I asked Freud: "How come?" and Freud said: "I was treating Gustav Mahler, and Mahler told me that he had accepted an engagement to be conductor in Hungary for the next year. And since I knew that Walter's pain in his arm was directly connected with the fact that he wanted very much to conduct, but that the only time he had the chance to conduct was when Mahler was ill, his arm would hurt him. It was a kind of penance he paid for unconsciously wishing Mahler would be ill so that he could conduct, and for enjoying conducting. So he paid his penance by having his arm hurt while he conducted."

By the way, Bruno Walter's name really was Schlesinger. He told me that he had to change it, for how would it sound to say: "Die Meistersinger conducted by Schlesinger." It was such a Jewish name, and the Austrians were terrible anti-Semites. Eventually Walter was also baptized. One can understand that.

❧

DR. REIK: We were talking about Einstein.

DR. FREEMAN: In a sense they both revolutionized the world, Einstein in outer space and Freud in inner space.

DR. REIK: Also, I told you that Freud complained that

people look at him as if he were an animal in a cage, in a zoo, and Einstein said: "I appear to myself like a whore. Everybody wants to know what I'm doing all the time and everyone wants to criticize me." In a letter to Einstein, Freud wrote: "My ideas would have been more easily accepted and more kindly had they contained more error in thought." He told me that when he first presented his lectures on hysteria before the college of physicians in Vienna, they roared with laughter. And one of them jumped up and said: "Mistake! Hysteria has to do only with women."

But Freud thought men could be hysterical too. Compared to Freud, Einstein was an optimist. Freud was a pessimist. Freud said: "At the end when the mind finally gets at peace, the body acts up." He was a cancer victim, of course. You know the quote of Konrad Ferdinand Meyer: "That is because I'm not a man out of fiction, but I am a man with his own contradiction." Freud quoted that very often.

DR. FREEMAN: Of course, Einstein found acceptance a lot sooner than Freud did.

DR. REIK: Much more, too, as a matter of fact.

Freud and Einstein had another peculiarity in common, namely, they liked Jewish jokes. I give you a joke of Freud. During the war, it was said about the Poles that they sell their country, but they don't deliver it. So it comes out that they are still patriots, because they sell it and they don't deliver it.

I have here also a note about Einstein. It is from the book of Michaelson. Einstein said that "the pursuit of knowledge for its own sake, and the almost fanatical love of justice, and the desire for personal independence, these are the features of the Jewish tradition which make me thank my lucky star that I belong to it."

DR. FREEMAN: And Freud was also proud of being Jewish?

DR. REIK: Yes. But Freud and Einstein both believed that there was a historical person Jesus.

⚜

DR. FREEMAN: You mentioned somewhere that Freud was a masochist and a great man.

DR. REIK: Yes, that was so. But I do not mean that in order for him to become great that the masochism was necessary. No. I mean that the abruptness, for instance, with which he broke with Fliess or with Breuer or with some of his students was self-damaging. You need not be abrupt. Think of Beethoven. Beethoven offended everyone—but just everybody. Or Brahms. Once Brahms was at a party and there was some critical talk about music. He got up and said: "If I have missed offending someone who is present, I apologize."

But it started from Jesus. th's masochistic trend, and we saw it in—what was the name of that Hungarian doctor who dea't with child delivery?

DR. FREEMAN: Semmelweis?

DR. REIK: Yes, Semmelweis. He got into such a fight with his colleagues that they should wash their hands when they helped with a delivery. And he broke with them. So I don't say that masochism is necessary to make a man great. But perhaps greatness brings masochism. I really think that there is no great man who was not a masochist. Mozart perhaps. No, even he was.

By the way, there was this Dr. Werner Jareck. Do you know the Jareck stories? He was the greatest enemy of Freud, the opponent. When Freud was seventy years old he got a telegram of congratulations from him signed, "Your most loyal opponent." Freud went on the rounds in the hospital with Jareck and the other doctors. And once they came to a psychotic patient and Freud said: "Look here, the sensorium of the patient is not disturbed. I'll demonstrate it to you." He asked the patient: "Where are you now?" The patient answered: "I'm in the hospital.' "And who are these gentlemen?" Freud asked. "They are all doctors," he said. "And who am I?" "You are an idiot." And Freud turned to the others doctors: "You see, I told you he's not crazy."

ANALYSTS

DR. FREEMAN: When you look at analysis as a field, would you say that it should be a semi-hard science or could you look at it as a kind of *Wahrheit und Dichtung?* In other words, how much of his own self—not only his training but his own intuitive conceptualization—does the analyst have to bring to what the patient is saying or doing, in order to find the truth?

DR. REIK: Yes, that's quite right, he brings quite a lot. But don't forget he must not take on himself the troubles of the patient. He must not introject the patient into himself. He only has to have a small taste of what the patient goes through. The potentiality for feeling all problems must be in him, so that nothing human is alien to him.

DR. FREEMAN: In other words, it's as if the analyst uses himself and his own emotions as a kaleidoscope . . .

DR. REIK: Yes.

DR. FREEMAN: . . . and sees their many little patterns, strains . . .

DR. REIK: Quite good.

DR. FREEMAN: . . . so that when you have a patient, you blow up one of those colors that corresponds to the patient's problem, and the analyst recognizes the pattern, without using all the patterns of his kaleidoscope.

DR. REIK: Yes. That's quite true. He analyzes the other person as if the other person were himself, and he analyzes himself as if he were another person, in self-analysis.

DR. FREEMAN: What kind of person should become a psychoanalyst?

DR. REIK: He should be sincere. And truthful, and when circumstances make it necessary, direct. By the way, that's not the way of women, in general. Women have to overcome the sex barrier to do that.

DR. FREEMAN: What do you mean, women are not direct?

DR. REIK: Women use diplomacy; they are not direct.

DR. FREEMAN: Not even with other women?

DR. REIK: With other women they can be. Even there they are not always.

DR. FREEMAN: In other words, directness is one trait an analyst needs?

DR. REIK: It depends on the situation. It's almost a technique, isn't it?

DR. FREEMAN: Can you separate the technique from the person?

DR. REIK: Yes, to a certain extent.

DR. FREEMAN: For instance?

DR. REIK: For instance, it seems that I have no talent for education.

DR. FREEMAN: You mean to educate someone else?

DR. REIK: Yes, I have no talent, it seems. And analysis

in certain cases is re-education. Espec'ally with certain
kinds of people, for people who have gone astray, and
so on. And I have to force myself to do something with
this kind of thing. For instance, when someone is close to
me, like my daughters, I don't think analytic—l'ke most
people. You want to, but you don't look at it that way.
So you don't see what is written there. So you see by
nature I am not a person who is an educator. But I use
the technique of education. On the other hand one can
also use one's personality. For instance, Freud sent me
a patient because he said I had, too, a little of what
Bergler later on called "psychic masoch'sm"—working
against my own interests and so on. And Freud said:
"that will help you help that patient." Because, of course,
I could understand him very well. One should use all
one's knowledge for analysis. I'll give another instance.
I was very witty as a boy, as a young man in my twenties
and when I studied psychology. I wrote *feuilletons* in
order to support myself. Do you know what *feuilletons*
are? They are articles, long articles which are in a news-
paper, and they were very witty. And then I came to Freud
and I asked him what should I do about that? And he said
I should suppress the writing. I should turn that facility
into analyt'c observation.

Dr. Freeman: What other qualities do you think an
analyst should have?

Dr. Reik: I would say an analyst should have what
Freud said, the courage to face unpleasant truths in himself
and in those around him. For instance, I have treated many
people who were intellectually superior to me. Some years
ago I treated a Nobel Prize physicist. The man could
th'nk rings around me. But I had one advantage over him,
besides my knowledge of analytic matters. The fact that
I had already faced myself.

Also, I think characterologically that an analyst should have a certain kind of emotional or social masochism, because he has to make great sacrifices for his science.

DR. FREEMAN: What kind of sacrifices?

DR. REIK: Financial; and sacrifices in time and the restriction of his society, because at least then, when we were a pioneer generation, we mixed almost only among ourselves.

DR. FREEMAN: Because you were not accepted on the outside?

DR. REIK: Not as analysts.

DR. FREEMAN: Do you think that young analysts today are as much concerned with their art, with their craft, as you were?

DR. REIK: No. We were fanatic. That means that we were preoccupied with the idea much more than they are now. There is this *pénétration pacifique*, a general dispersion of analysis—everybody knows about it now. And that was not the case then.

DR. FREEMAN: Do you think it does the young analyst harm because he is not so deeply immersed in it? Or is it better for him to diversify his interests?

DR. REIK: Yes, I'd say it is better not to be so concentrated as we were. Freud, for instance, in his later years preferred not to mix so much with analysts privately. He mixed very much with writers and with archeologists and with people of other kinds.

But Freud showed me a letter which he got from a doctor in Holland. This doctor wrote to Freud that he has given up psychiatric practice in order to become a psychoanalyst, which is what he is now. And Freud said: "That man is now married, because being an analyst is a destiny. It hangs together with the character."

DR. FREEMAN: Becoming an analyst is a destiny?

DR. REIK: Yes. It has something to do with the character of a person.

DR. FREEMAN: Was the psychiatrist writing to be praised?

DR. REIK: Yes, he wanted to be praised.

Now again about tests of what makes a psychoanalyst. The interest in analysis is various. In therapy, in pedagogics, in application of anthropology, religion. But the general term under which it comes is that the interest in psychoanalysis is psychological. There must be a certain common denominator which determines why one becomes an analyst. At Vienna University there are statues of famous men in the courtyard, for instance, of Professor Notnagel. And below that statue it has one of his sayings which was, "*Nur ein guter Mensch can ein guter Artz sein.*" [Only a good human being can be a good doctor.] When you interpret that analytically it means only a man who has conquered and sublimated and overcome his sadistic drives, "ein *guter* Mensch," can become a good physician. One of the distinctive components for this choice of profession is, of course, the wish to attempt to heal and to cure—wh'ch goes back to the overcoming of the original cruelty in us.

In the courtyard at Vienna University is also the bust of Freud with the quotation from Sophocles' *Oedipus*, "He solved the riddle of the sphinx." You know what is the riddle of the sphinx: "What walks on four legs in the morning, on two in the afternoon, and on three in the evening?" The answer is "Man"—on four is the baby crawling, on two is the adult, on three is the old person with a cane. So Freud solved the riddle of the sphinx.

To go on with this question of what makes a psychoanalyst, let us assume that it could be proven that by hormone or medical treatment of endocrine secretion the neurosis and the psychosis could be cured in a few days. Namely, you discover that the neurosis and psychosis are conditions determined by certain *Energieverwendungen*—that is to say, displacement of emotional energy—which depends entirely on endocrine processes and which can be changed by hormones or medications. From then on, neurosis and psychosis are treated only by means of endocrine changes, and the practical as well as theoretical interest is on the physiological aspects only.

If now a physician continues h's interest in neurosis, then I would say he is an excellent physician, but he is not a psychoanalyst. Meaning that if he were a psychoanalyst then he would be interested in *psychological* problems. He would turn his interest away from the physiolog'cal problems and processes, and he would transfer his interest to other emotional and mental phenomena. Correct, hm? I, for my mortal part at least, would do that. So that would be one test in thought.

I take as a point of departure some of the sayings of Freud. In June 1938, that means less than one year before his death, he wrote about psychoanalysis for the Encyclopaedia Britannica. In that he said that it is clear that in the future endocrinology will have a decisive word to say about the neurosis and psychosis. He foresaw the phys'cal things of what is now known about tranquilizers and hormones in the treatment of these diseases. But he said that at that time we could fight them with psychological means. In his lectures, which I remember well, especially the later ones, he said that psychoanalysis and endocrinology are to be compared to two groups of workers who are digg'ng a tunnel from both sides and who will meet in the middle. That is a very nice comparison, no? And if we assume now for a moment that endocrinology—of which, incidentally, he said in another connection: "I hear the steps of endocrinology behind me"—if we assume a situation in which endocrinology gets ahead and lands before the other at the middle of the tunnel—and convinces us without any doubt that neurosis and psychosis are only conditioned by *Energie-verschiebungen*, which are physiological—then I, and everyone elese who feels himself a psychoanalyst, would get away from his interest in the neurosis and psychosis and would become interested in other things that are emotional or mental processes.

On the other hand, if a genius would come later than Freud and would convince me that we can have a new psychological approach that's much better or much more penetrating to the unconsc'ous processes than analysis, I would immediately be interested in that. It means, in other words, once a psychologist, always a psychologist.

DR. FREEMAN: What about the difference in the culture, in the kind of background and education that a European analyst has had when he treats an American patient?

DR. REIK: There is something in that because we Europeans had to make ourselves acquainted with myths, with literature, with religion. And that is missed very often in the education of American medical analysts. Though not in all American analysts.

DR. FREEMAN: Now that more is known about psychoanalysis, patients tend to ask what school do you belong to?

DR. REIK: There are no schools, I would answer. I think I told you that someone called me up and said: "We are the representatives here of Freudian psychoanalysis." And I said: "Is there any other?" Freud himself knew, of course, about the Horney group, who emphasize the sociological point of view. And Freud always said when he was talking about them: "I do not doubt that they are excellent sociologists. But the task of psychoanalysis is a very restricted and modest one. Analysis has to deal with the unconscious—not only with the unconscious-repressed but with the unconscious in general—and its connection with the conscious thinking and conscious feelings. That is the narrow field of psychoanalysis." And about these sociologists he said: "It would be unfair to expect that we who are only psychologists should also deal with sociological, economic, and other aspects of life, which no doubt have a great influence." He said we have to leave that to others. And he used another of his comparisons: "It would be as unfair as if in a concert orchestra, you expect that the man who plays the fiddle should at the same time play the trombone. The man is only a violinist, and only when all work together, play together, each his own instrument, can a symphony be performed. It is unfair to expect that an excellent fiddler must play the trombone."

❦

DR. FREEMAN: Did you know Alfred Adler?

DR. REIK: Yes, certainly.

DR. FREEMAN: What was he like?

DR. REIK: He was gemütlich. You know, Adler was Jewish, yet he spoke in a strong Viennese dialect, which was a little funny to us. It was very interesting. It was not the way any of us spoke.

DR. FREEMAN: You mean Adler used the working class dialect?

DR. REIK: Yes, deliberately. Don't forget there is a difference. This broad dialect was spoken by two classes. First by the lower classes in Vienna and also by the higher aristocrats. But not the middle class or the intelligentsia. I think Adler had a feeling of inferiority and was influenced by that. He was also a Socialist, and an urgent one, a passionate one, which I think is one of the reasons he spoke in the dialect of the working class.

Later on he became hostile to Freud, because Adler discovered, for instance, that all neuroses are the same deep down. But Freud had already said that at the Vienna Psychoanalytic Society. Adler once said to Freud: *"Ich habe keine Lust ewig in Ihrem Schatten zustehen."* How you would translate that? "I don't relish standing in your shadow forever." So you see, there was a competition which was furious.

Besides that his dedication to socialism, so to speak, colored his personality, caused him to be more interested in political things than he perhaps as an analyst should have been. So he had these revolutionary tendencies and they had some influence upon his teaching, too. For instance, the *Weibliche* Protest, the *Männliche* Protest which he speaks about, by which he means that the woman is always in protest against the man. Good. But then he said that the protest expresses itself even in the tendency of the woman to lie on top of the man. Which contradicts all clinical human experience—generally women prefer the other position. From there he thought that in the positions of sexual intercourse, the woman should always be on top of the husband, the man. And that when she was underneath him it is because she was economically dependent upon him.

DR. FREEMAN: What did he say was the origin of neurosis?

DR. REIK: That's also where Freud and he disagreed. They both said every neurosis had the same origin. But Adler said that it was all *Organminderwertigkeit.* He said certain organs are considered inferior by a person, and he tries to overcome this by achieving even more because of it. Like Demosthenes, who couldn't speak properly

and forced himself to overcome that difficulty by prac-
ticing to speak with little stones in his mouth. So Adler's
contribution is also the concept of inferiority. Also sibling
rivalry.

DR. FREEMAN: Wilhelm Reich?

DR. REIK: Wilhelm Reich was a very gifted man,
especially in the early days when he wrote about the neurotic character. And when he wrote about the function
of the orgasm, there still were certain good insights there.
But later on he came, of course, with his orgone therapy,
and then he thought he could cure cancer. As you know
he died in prison hospital. His daughter is a psychoanalyst
now. He and I were in the same analytic society. Once
he gave a lecture at a Congress, and I said to him at the
end of the lecture: "But look, that is something which
I have always said," and he said: "No, Herr Doktor Reik,
we differ decidedly." And from then on he was very
cool toward me, and hostile. He had a certain paranoid
trend; he thought himself persecuted.

DR. FREEMAN: What was the idea you told him you
had also said?

DR. REIK: It was about character armor. That a character surrounds himself with a certain armor to be pro-
tected. And what I said before was quite similar. It wasn't
the same, but similar.

DR. FREEMAN: And he resented the fact that you mentioned it to him?

DR. REIK: Yes.

DR. FREEMAN: Why was Karl Abraham against lay
analysis?

DR. REIK: He was a physician, and he was on principle
against it. Don't forget, Abraham died in 1925, so it was of
the time. All the Americans were against it then, too.

DR. FREEMAN: What was their principle?

DR. REIK: It should only be reserved for physicians. But Abraham had nothing against analyzing me if I gave myself to applied analysis—the work of Hans Sachs and Otto Rank.

DR. FREEMAN: What did Abraham mean by applied analysis?

DR. REIK: Applied means history, religion, comparative mythology.

DR. FREEMAN: As opposed to treating patients?

DR. REIK: Yes, only physicians should treat patients. But personally we were on excellent terms, despite our conflicting opinions. When Abraham died, I gave the eulogy at the Vienna Analytic Society.

DR. FREEMAN: Did you know Eitinger?

DR. REIK: Yes. Eitinger left Germany early and went to Palestine. And my son, who went there, too, chose him as a father representative, so to speak, while I was in Europe and in America. Eitinger had a house in Jerusalem which was entirely like his house in Berlin. He had taken all his things with him. I think he was still a Russian citizen at that time. His wife was an actress from the Moscow Theater. He stammered, by the way, Eitinger. He was shy and very, very clever. A highly intelligent man. Very rich originally. His relatives were great fur merchants in Leipzig and in Russia.

DR. FREEMAN: What about Otto Rank?

DR. REIK: Rank was originally a student of the technical high school in Vienna. He wrote about *Lohengrin* there.

DR. FREEMAN: How did you meet him?

DR. REIK: At first I met him, of course, at the Psycho-

analytical Society. Then later he and Hans Sachs and I
became friends, and they called us in Berlin the psychoanalytic trio. For a time Rank, Sachs, and I were the only
lay analysts in Vienna.

Rank's name was originally Rosenfeld, and then he took
the name of "Rank" from Ibsen.

DR. FREEMAN: Did he like the theater very much?

DR. REIK: No, no. But he read a lot about the motif
of incest, you know, in which he followed all the expressions of incestuous motives in the whole literature and
so he came to Ibsen, too, of course.

DR. FREEMAN: But it was not because of his love for
the theater.

DR. REIK: No.

DR. FREEMAN: I think the incest motif was very well
put in Konrad Ferdinand Meyer's *Die Richterin*.

DR. REIK: Yes. Rank mentioned that too.

Freud originally thought everything of Rank. He had
the highest opinion of him, and Rank was very, very
gifted, very gifted. I saw a letter which Freud wrote to
a patient in which he recommended Rank, and said: "He
knows perhaps more than I do about psychoanalysis." So,
when Rank wrote the *Incest Motif* and his first book, *The
Lohengrin Saga*, he had something which I lacked: he had
elbow strength, drive. I said to Freud once that if Rank
would have entered Gerngross, which was like Macy's, if
he had begun there as a clerk, he would have ended as
vice president, you know? On account of his energy and
this push he had. He couldn't be exhausted by work; he
worked twenty hours a day. After his analytic hours, he
sat down and wrote. He used every one. But when Rank
came to America, America spoiled him. He began to play
the stock exchange, he got rich. It reminds me of what my
grandfather always said: "*Kovet rechts und Kasse links.*"
"Go to the right for honor, and to the left for money."

And in the meantime, Rank had written *The Trauma of Birth*. Rank gave the trauma of birth central place in psychoanalysis. He said it was the most important thing in the whole analysis. And Freud disagreed with that entirely. Also, with Rank's interpretation of dreams.

Freud was perhaps more wounded by Rank's leaving him, than by the conflict with him. From some conversations I had with Freud, I sometimes had the impression that he considered it his destiny that some of his best pupils would leave him. There was Ferenzci, Jung, Adler, Rank. They all dropped away.

Rank first went to Paris. He stayed in Paris for a while, and then he came to America.

DR. FREEMAN: Did he stay here for the rest of his life?

DR. REIK: Yes, he died here.

DR. FREEMAN: Why did he come to America?

DR. REIK: He was called here by a patient. He was here from 1934 to 1939.

DR. FREEMAN: So America had only five years of him.

DR. REIK: Yes, but in that time, he made a fortune. He played the stock market, as I told you, and he got divorced from his wife.

DR. REIK: A very interesting case was Steckel, because at first he was quite perceptive, and quite progressive, and then he became a little what I called the "wild psychoanalyst."

DR. FREEMAN: Wild?

DR. REIK: He practiced wild psychoanalysis, in his dream interpretations and in every other direction. Pure guesswork, you know, for which there is no objective proof. Freud didn't like Steckel.

DR. FREEMAN: Why?

DR. REIK: Because of Steckel's dream interpretations, I guess. Also, whenever we had a session in the analytic association, he always had a patient ready who he said had *that* and *that* and *that*.

DR. FREEMAN: Did you like him?

DR. REIK: No, I didn't like him very much.

One of the most interesting relationships which Freud had was with Ferenczi, who was his closest friend over the years. Ferenczi thought that people who become neurotic had too little love as children, and he tried to give them love. That means, he petted them, he put a woman or a man on his lap. He talked baby talk with them. He treated the patients, grownups, as if they were children. And Freud said: "Where is the bed? You cannot do that with them." Freud believed that analysis has to be led in abstinence for the patient. That means, just that which the patient mostly wants, namely the love of the analyst, he should not get. The patient should repeat the disappointments he had as a child in order to work it through and overcome it. From the analyst he should get only interest in his welfare.

DR. FREEMAN: But did Ferenczi have any results?

DR. REIK: Of course. For the moment it works, it's very soothing to a patient. But only temporarily. I talk about that in my book, *The Need to be Loved*.

And then came the break—Ferenczi got ill. He got leukemia, and then died. That was also very painful to Freud.

DR. FREEMAN: What was Ernest Jones like?

DR. REIK: He was very nice. And he was very typically British. I'll give you an example. Jones came to Vienna, it was in the early days. From Vienna he wanted to go to the French Riviera for fourteen days, and so had to go to the French Embassy. He didn't know his way around, of course. I was at Freud's, and I said to Jones:

"I'll go with you, I'll take you there so you won't have any difficulty with the language"—because I had studied French, you know? We went to the Embassy and we were led to the Consul, and I began to explain the situation in French. And while I talked, a word eluded me. So Jones, who sat beside me and hadn't said a word, began to talk. And he spoke much better French than I. He said: "I speak French, but not very well," and he spoke it better than I.

DR. FREEMAN: Who were the people in the Wednesday Circle?

DR. REIK: The ones we just talked about. Also Titschman and sometimes Silberer. Jones often came to Vienna; Titschman sat beside me and intoned: "Baruch atoh adonai, here comes the honor Goy." Of course, we were all Jews.

DR. FREEMAN: All except Jung?

DR. REIK: Jung was not in Vienna, he lived in Switzerland. He traveled to Vienna sometimes and he came to Congresses, but he didn't come to the meetings. Jones sometimes did come to the meetings from London.

Apropos Jung and Jones. Once Jung did not inform Jones of a special meeting and Freud was angry with Jung for that. And I said to Freud: "He only forgot. After all it is unconscious." And Freud answered: "A gentleman wouldn't have an unconscious like that!"

DR. FREEMAN: Did you know Jung?

DR. REIK: Oh, yes, certainly.

DR. FREEMAN: What did you think of him?

DR. REIK: I didn't like him, but Freud liked him very much.

DR. FREEMAN: Why didn't you like him?

DR. REIK: Because he was too Goyish.

DR. FREEMAN: Too Goyish? In what way?

Dr. Reik: Oh, he talked very, very loud, and very decisive, authoritative. He was blond and tall. . . .

Dr. Freeman: And why did Freud like him?

Dr. Reik: Freud felt attracted to him at first. He came from Switzerland, you know? Freud liked him very much.

Dr. Freeman: Was there any reason why he liked him?

Dr. Reik: No. I think he was attracted to him originally, because Freud was small, you know, and Jewish-looking, don't forget.

Jung published his autobiography in which he gives his teaching. He landed at the idea that the incest taboo is not of interest—it's not the mother. And he denies the importance of sex, in the sense of Freud. That was the real core of the conflict between them. He said sex is not so important.

Dr. Freeman: What did he say is important?

Dr. Reik: Prime images—the animus and the anima. And they are gotten from the racial unconscious.

I remember that at first Freud hoped that Jung would eventually take over his place. But Freud had to give that idea up, and that hurt him very much.

Jung was prejudiced against Jews. It seemed as though he had given it up entirely when he came to Freud, but that was not correct. Freud told me sometimes that he hoped Jung would give up racial prejudices and that he would give up his anti-Semitism. Jung was the son of a pastor, and that had an influence upon his teaching. He did not give up his anti-Semitism.

Dr. Freeman: How did Jung's anti-Semitism or racial prejudice manifest itself?

Dr. Reik: I don't know anything about that; but later he welcomed Hitler and became dedicated to the Nazis. He thought there was a Jewish psychology and a German Christian psychology.

Dr. Freeman: And did he say what the difference was?

Dr. Reik: Yes, he said that psychoanalysis, in the sense of Freud, is Jewish psychology. And he, Jung, represented the German Christian psychology, so to speak. Some psychoanalysts later on said that the idea was not without influence, that Jung was the sum of all those parts.

The interesting story, the opposite story, is that of Fromm, Erich Fromm. He was at first opposed to Freud. Originally Fromm was studying to be a rabbi. Then he moved away from that and yet he remained really Jewish in his main taste and character—he remains somewhere religious. He has a nice sense of humor. Once he asked me for an address and the number of the street was very high; something like 2340. And to that Fromm said: *"Unberufen."* How would you translate that? "May he continue to have success," or something. Very nice. He became a student of Karen Horney.

Dr. Freeman: Did you know Horney?

Dr. Reik: Oh, I knew her very well.

Dr. Freeman: What was she like?

Dr. Reik: Horney was very nice. She was a very pretty girl. Blonde and blue-eyed, a little like you. She was the prototype of the German girl, although she was really Scandinavian. She was a forceful woman. We were both students of Karl Abraham in Berlin. At that time, she had not yet developed the sociological approach. Horney was quite gifted as a sociologist you know? And she certainly in some directions had ideas which were justified. Freud did not deny that the school of Horney had its merits—as sociologists, but not as psychologists. He said that sociology would be our field as analysts, too, if the area between the unconscious and the conscious supported it. But the idea of social influences in the building up of neurosis is wrong—it's quite clear. Well, then, it is not our field. He said it would be unfair if we would do that. We should restrict ourselves; we are much more modest in our field.

DR. FREEMAN: Did you know the Princess Marie Bonaparte?

DR. REIK: Oh, yes. I liked her very much. She was a highly intelligent and very beautiful woman. She was a very well-known psychoanalyst in France. Her writings on female sexuality are excellent.

Freud had a remarkable relationship with Marie Bonaparte. She was always there. She was rather eccentric, and she had a very strange peculiarity: wherever she went, she would lie down. We invited her once for dinner and she came and she was lying down, immediately. She talked better that way. She was a very wonderful woman. Full of spirit. She died an old lady not so long ago.

A funny thing happened with her. One day the princess and I were at the library at the University and she wanted to take a book home. But one could not take books from the University library, so she asked me to introduce her to the Director of the library. So I brought her into his office and introduced him and she said: "I am Marie Bonaparte." And the Director said: "Take a chair." And she said: "But I am Princess Marie Bonaparte." The Director said: "Take two chairs."

She was quite a woman. She helped to save Freud, to ransom him from the Nazis. She always had her shoes off, and she was always lying down.

DR. FREEMAN: She could sit, but thank God she didn't have to.

DR. REIK: How do you mean?

DR. FREEMAN: You know, the story about the protective mother who took her son with her to Florida for the winter. When they arrived in her car at the hotel, she asked the bell captain to have her son carried upstairs. So he sent two bellhops out to carry the boy to his room. Then he turned to the mother and said solicitously: "How old is your son?" And the mother answered, "Thirteen." "I'm so sorry," said the bell captain, "that he can't walk." And the mother turned to him and said: "What do you mean? Of course he can walk—but thank God he doesn't have to."

DR. FREEMAN: Was there a difference between the German psychoanalysts and the Viennese?

DR. REIK: Only in their pronunciation.

Freud used to tell a little story from the First World War about the difference between the Germans and the Viennese. In Galicia, a cannon got stuck in the mud. It couldn't move, and the men of the Viennese regiment went there and said "Uh-uh-oh-go-the-gun," and the cannon didn't move. Then a German regiment passed by, and the lieutenant saw that the Viennese were having trouble with the cannon. So the German lieutenant said: "Oh, you sloppy Viennese, I'll show you." He took ten men and put their shoulders to the cannon and he commanded, "One, two, three!" And they pushed the cannon out of the mud. And the Viennese soldiers that were there said, "*Na ja, mit Gewalt,*" which means, "Well, of course, if you use force . . ." Freud liked that story very much. *Na ja, mit Gewalt . . .*

MEN AND WOMEN

Dr. Freeman: How would one define femininity and masculinity?

Dr. Reik: We cannot define it.

Dr. Freeman: We cannot?

Dr. Reik: Freud said something about that in the second part of his lectures.

Dr. Freeman: In other words, what we consider masculine and feminine is a cultural definition?

Dr. Reik: Yes, cultural, you could say that. Besides anatomical, of course. Freud quoted Napoleon: "Anatomy is destiny."

Dr. Freeman: Well, have you found that there is a difference between the kind of communication of a male patient to a female analyst, and a male patient to a male analyst—the kind of relationship that develops and the kind of material that is brought out. Isn't there a difference in what comes first . . . ?

Dr. Reik: Yes, correct. I once had a young woman

patient who had a violent and sexual transference to me—
I was much younger then. But she did not want to show
that, and instead got into a quarrel with me and left. She
went downstairs and came back. But a man would not
come back—he would leave and be finished. The second
thing would be the following: there is scarcely anything
to be compared with the resistance of a man against homosexuality, that is, offering himself to another man. There
is scarcely anything in a woman which is that strong.
But a man patient can have fantasies of having a child of
a male analyst, and so putting himself entirely in the
feminine.

DR. FREEMAN: Men do have such fantasies, but they
tend strongly to resist them?

DR. REIK: Yes. In general I would say that from a
certain age on in a boy, the fantasy of being a girl meets
a very strong resistance. I sometimes, in analysis, try to
see if it is possible for a patient to remember such fantasies. I say: "What is so wrong with it? It is a fantasy
as if I were President of the United States, or if I were
a slave. I can have all kinds of fantasies. Why should
I not have fantasies of being a girl?"

I know, of course, boys who were very jealous of girls.
I have a patient who was jealous of girls when he was
young, because he always felt that a boy has to go to the
girl to ask for a date, and so on, while a girl can sit with
her hands in her lap and wait. So there is also a resistance
to taking over the active aggressive role.

DR. FREEMAN: And with women?

DR. REIK: There is an educational difference. Freud
said that it is all nonsense to deny it. He said to me that
a woman who offers herself to a man, a man analyst, has a
great charm. Because generally women do not offer themselves sexually.

Dr. Freeman: So the fact that she is offering herself is a charm in itself.

Dr. Reik: Yes, for the analyst. But he has, of course, to control that . . . I remember a patient came to me from Australia. I remember that because she considered herself a colonial, and she spoke with a certain accent which was not British. Freud referred her to me. We started analysis, and in the middle—it was after the first five or six weeks—she couldn't say a word, although I encouraged her to say what she could. She was tongue-tied. She couldn't say a word. She didn't come the next time, and instead went to see Freud. Freud called me and let me come over to him, and he told me what prevented her from talking to me. When she was in Sydney, she had some kind of gynecological troubles, and she was going to a young gynecologist. She was on an examining table when the gynecologist made a pass at her. Now, she was lying on the couch, and that was the fantasy she had, so she couldn't continue speaking further.

Then she came back to me and discussed it openly, and she got over it. And she told me the last dream she had. At this time, that was more than forty years ago, there were the first gramophones, and she had a dream that she was aboard ship going home to Australia and heard a gramophone with a record of my voice. So she took me home, the voice of me. So that ended on a very nice note. It was quite a good analysis at the time.

Dr. Freeman: Do you think there is something to this myth that it is better if you are married to have a woman analyst?

Dr. Reik: It makes no difference. I would say that is true if there is an emphasized, strong hostility against all women. Then the analyst should be a woman so the patient can reconcile himself to whatever is the conflict with his mother or his sister.

DR. FREEMAN: Suppose a male analyst gets a patient who has a very strong hostility towards women. He would not necessarily send him to a female analyst, would he?

DR. REIK: No. But I would not have any objections to sending him.

DR. FREEMAN: Are there indications sometimes?

DR. REIK: Only if there is a continual hostility, towards all women. Not only his mother or his sister, but to all women.

DR. REIK: What do you think of that young lady you just met?

DR. FREEMAN: She's a nice girl.

DR. REIK: I'm glad you don't like her either. You know, women have a way of insulting each other while they compliment one another. Freud once told me about a witty actress who said to someone she met at a party: "One hears so many terrible things about you, one hopes they are all true." And I heard one woman say to another: "You look so pretty today, I scarcely recognized you."

I'll tell you something which not I, but Dr. Sulzberger, found out about women in contrast to men. He asserts that women communicate with each other with glances, and men not. Let's say the following: you are somewhere with your husband and some women friends. Someone says something, and you look at a woman friend and you have communicated a certain thing. Dr. Sulzberger says that women have a "conspiratorial whisper" amongst themselves. "Conspiratorial whisper" comes from psychiatric language. It means a paranoic thinks that people whisper together about him. And women, so Sulzberger says, when they are together with men and they want to say something to other women so that men shouldn't hear, they have a conspiratorial whisper. There is a kind of secret language in this. When I was a boy, that means twelve, thirteen, we found out that women have together a secret language. A group of girls wanted to make an excursion in the Vienna Woods. They'd say: "Let's make it for Thursday," and this one girl would say: "No, Thursday, I can't. My aunt is coming." That meant that she will be menstruating. A student of mine in Vienna wrote a paper and I gave her some hints and helped her a little about the different language of men and women. You know that men, for instance, very rarely say "cute," except when they are homosexuals, or "so sweet." Homosexuals do that when they make fun of women. I heard homosexuals speak among themselves, and one said to the other: "I tell you, let's take a basket and go to market, you look so cute, darling." That means he made fun of the language that embarrassed him. Women don't say: "You are so cute, sweetie," to each other.

It is also true that when a man says a lie, he is somewhere uncomfortable. When a woman says a lie she is very placid and self-confident. In one of my books, I pointed to a subtle demonstration of that: Two men speak to each other in the bus—let's say about the stock exchange or business. They have said what they have to say and they are silent, especially when they don't want to discuss a certain thing. When women come to a point where they don't want to discuss a certain thing, they change the subject of their conversation. But they keep talking. That begins very early. A woman patient made me aware of that. She had a son and a daughter, and when she says to the boy: "What are you thinking?" he makes an unwilling gesture or says: "Leave me alone," or such, if he doesn't want to say what he was thinking. While the girl says: "I just thought my doll should have a new dress." She finds a way out very quickly. She says something else, not what she really thought. So there are differences early.

Dr. Freeman: As patients, generally what is the difference between men and women—or is there a difference to begin with?

Dr. Reik: Certainly, good. I would say in the first interview, you, the analyst, can be different with men and women. You will in the first interview be less direct with women; you use better words. And you will only ask, for instance, about sex when you feel that the woman has overcome a certain shyness about talking about it. If she is then willing to talk about sex, it shows you already that she has in fact overcome that shyness.

Then you have to be aware of the following: that when men are shy, in general they show it. When women are shy, they disguise it, much better than men. Women are better actors. Remember that famous story of Lady Astor? Lady Astor was the first woman who was giving a speech in the House of Lords, or maybe it was in the House of Commons, I don't know. It was more than forty years ago. She got up and spoke very freely and eloquently before this most prominent assembly of men. After, her lady friends came to congratulate her and then she took one of her friends aside and said: "What a blessing it is that we women have long skirts, because that way no one could see that my knees were trembling all the time." That is typical.

Dr. Freeman: How do men indicate their shyness?

Dr. Reik: They cannot disguise it so well. I give you an instance. In the first interview I would never ask a woman whether she is shy. I could ask her whether she was shy as a girl, in her puberty years and so on. But I could ask a man directly: "Are you generally shy?" and: "Were you shy as a boy, too? How is it with you when you meet an important man in your business? Are you shy with him? Does it depend on the reaction of the person with whom you talk? With whom are you more shy, with women or with men?" That gives an indication.

DR. FREEMAN: What if there is a shyness that is equal in both cases, with men and with women?

DR. REIK: Usually there is no such thing.

DR. FREEMAN: For instance, one of my women patients —her shyness is equal in both cases. She is afraid of men and of women, and shy with both. She shudders when she has to meet either a man or a woman.

DR. REIK: I would say that behavior is an exceptional case. Let's say, you are out together with women, and in a room. And then two other women come into the room. You don't give a damn—which you would if there were men. Or you would undress in front of women, no? There must be difference in the sex.

DR. FREEMAN: In the symptomatology, there is a difference.

DR. REIK: Oh, yes, I would say that. You could say there is a greater tendency of women to express an emotional process by physical symptoms. Not as often as before psychoanalysis, because by the dispersion of knowledge about hysteria, you see hardly any classical hysterics anymore. But there is still more of a tendency toward headaches or other pains in women than in men.

Now, there is another difference. That is the following: in general, we are searching for normal patterns of behavior, which are, so to speak, the subpatterns of pathological things. For instance, I have a case of a paranoiac, let's say, who thinks that all people observe him. There is a normal equivalent to that, which is not so pathological. And men in general are more often paranoid than women.

DR. FREEMAN: Partly because women are more accustomed to being looked at?

DR. REIK: Yes, because as little girls, they are more watched over by their mothers, and so expect that later.

DR. REIK: You know, women convinced against their feelings, are of the same opinion still. That means that with a woman you don't argue by using logic. For instance, for men A is not B. That means: If I like someone, it doesn't mean I don't like him. Women can like someone and dislike him at the same time. They have not what the Greeks call the "exclusion of the Third." They can have the one and the other at the same time. It is impossible for a man to understand that. I remember the following situation. A young man wooed a young girl and she was responding. Very nice. And then he was supposed to come to see her at ten, but he came early. She was very cool to him, absolutely rejecting. And from that came a conflict.

DR. FREEMAN: She was embarrassed.

DR. REIK: Yes. You know what she said when I talked with her? She said: "I had curlers in my hair when he came." He was an hour early and she was not dressed, and therefore she was in a bad mood. But from her point of view it is correct.

DR. FREEMAN: Because the female point of view is that it is more appearance than the fact of his presence?

DR. REIK: Yes. He, on the other hand, thought: "She doesn't like me anymore." He was looking for logical reasons why she was cool to him. A man must always take the chance that the woman is illogical.

DR. FREEMAN: Only from his point of view. But I always thought it is better to be logical. If the premise is correct then the syllogism follows.

DR. REIK: No, no. I quote Einstein. He said that in finding out and describing the truth, leave the elegance to the women. It is very good, "leave the elegance to the women."

DR. FREEMAN: But even if a woman's tendency is to be logical, she still is accused of being illogical, even when she is being logical.

DR. REIK: In her mind she is logical. Still, she shouldn't be logical.

DR. FREEMAN: Why not?

DR. REIK: She should think with her heart. Matthew Arnold wrote: "With Women the heart argues, not the mind." But it sometimes argues better.

DR. FREEMAN: But what does she say if a man says: "I can't talk to you, because you are not logical."

DR. REIK: Then I would tell her to answer: "Well, am I not a woman?"

❧

DR. FREEMAN: You have said that the lives of women have changed. In what ways do you thing that is so?

DR. REIK: In the pioneer age they shared the tasks of men—they even shot at the Indians that attacked. I would say that now they still share the life of their husbands to a certain extent, but not in their professional life. Women go out to work if it's needed, to businesses, offices, but they also return to their home responsibilities. Then when the children go beyond a certain age, then the lives of women become empty and meaningless. Very many women neglect what they have learned in their high school and college years, and don't make use of it.

DR. FREEMAN: They have been taught to think it's dangerous to make use of their brains. In this country, if you are a smart girl, you're supposed to hide it.

DR. REIK: Yes. I would say they avoid ostentatiously to go into competition with men with regard to brain power. Not always . . . some do. I told you that about

Madame Curie, no? Madame Curie discovered the X-rays.
She was a genius, undoubtedly. She was married to a
mediocre physicist who helped her, and when she came
back from Stockholm, where she got the Nobel Prize,
she was celebrated in the salons of Paris like a goddess.
Wherever she went she was praised as a great benefactor
of mankind. She said: *"Pas moi; c'est Pierre"*—Pierre, her
husband—and pushed him into the limelight.

DR. FREEMAN: You think perhaps that women, as they
are now cannot really help their husbands? So what may
happen is that if you have a relationship with someone
and can't cooperate with him, then you will compete
with him?

DR. REIK: No, you need not.

DR. FREEMAN: But in the early days, a woman stood
at the barricades . . .

DR. REIK: Yes.

DR. FREEMAN: . . . and she had a very well-defined
job, and her job was as essential to the protection of life
as his job was. Then they could work together. But now,
if the husband says: "I'm going to work—I have my work
and you sit home," then that's it.

DR. REIK: Yes, that's quite right, it's bad. I would say
the first, women who need for financial reasons go out
to offices—and how many do that?—and then cook dinner,
or take care of their children. Then in all the other fields
they need not compete because there are other kinds of
jobs for their husbands, no?

DR. FREEMAN: But competition—I don't mean it necessarily in the sense of competing for the same job, but competing for status . . .

DR. REIK: Yes, I pointed out in *The Need To Be Loved*,
that initially the girl and the boy have the same means
to impress their mothers or their fathers. But very soon,
the boy and the girl differentiate in this direction. Then

the girl should operate by her beauty and her charm and her personality, the boy by his achievement.

DR. FREEMAN: What if she has brains?

DR. REIK: Wait a moment. We speak about little boys and little girls. The little girl will dance around and show how charmingly she can do that. The boy will shout on his bicycle—"Look, Ma, without hands!" So, if that is correct, then I would say, it remains in life, for life, that the woman should affect people by her charm, by her beauty, and by her behavior, in short by her personality. And a man should impress by his achievements and accomplishments. I always say to my daughters: "A woman should affect men by her beauty—that means externally as well as internally, by her personality." One is never enough, because you think of this "dumb blonde" who is so attractive externally, but so what? I saw many, many women who failed to do that. I remember a patient of mine, who, when there was company, when she entertained people with her husband, she was always talking. Until I told her she should quit pushing into the limelight. *He* should be there, which is correct.

DR. FREEMAN: What happens to a girl who has been trained, whose brain . . .

DR. REIK: Well, why should she? Look at Madame Curie. She was certainly a genius.

DR. FREEMAN: And what is she to do with her brain?

DR. REIK: She should use it, certainly. But she should not be in competition with her husband.

DR. FREEMAN: But very often it is the husband who competes with the wife. And if the husbands are at the office, and the wives stay at home, and they feel that, in effect, they're just being used? They're fulfillers. And they're housekeepers, they live in the suburbs, away from where life really is. They have the tendency now to look for life, to do something . . .

Dr. Reik: Yes, that's quite right. Sometimes, women are —and that is very interesting—in general, jealous of the work of the man. That came to my consciousness in a film in which Noel Coward played. The film was *In Which We Serve*—it was during the war. And in the film you see that the wife is very jealous of the ship on which the man is captain. Now, the ship is itself a woman—you say "she" in English. It seems that is generally so. A Frenchman formulated once the following sentence: "One of the minor tragedies of life is that women love men, but men love work."

Dr. Freeman: Then in a sense, a woman experiences a man's work as her rival.

Dr. Reik: Yes, correct.

Dr. Freeman: So insofar as he says: "You stay out of my office," he's saying in effect: "You are the third part of a triangle, and intrude upon my affairs." In a sense, sometimes where a woman could be most helpful to a man, he doesn't really permit her to be.

Dr. Reik: No, I wouldn't say that.

Dr. Freeman: For instance, she's not allowed in the office, right?

Dr. Reik: He says, if she can type . . .

Dr. Freeman: . . . type. Big deal. Even so, the chances are he prefers his secretary. But outside of the office she is obligated to be his hostess.

Dr. Reik: Good, good. Someone once said about the woman: "She has many functions. She should be a lady in the parlor," something else I don't remember, I will have to look it up, "and a whore in bed."

Dr. Freeman: But suppose now she does his entertaining. The boss comes to dinner, or if he himself is the boss then she has to entertain for new clients. Is it in a sense, subconsciously, that she is helping her rival? I'm not speaking of the reality. But if his work is her rival, her social function at home, to get him more business, is in a sense aiding her own rival?

DR. REIK: Yes, she has to take that in her stride. On the other hand, you could say the following: The company of a man, that means what kind of people he entertains, depends on the woman. She invites. That means she decides her company . . . He could express his wishes, but she decides.

DR. FREEMAN: Except in terms of business, where she has no choice.

DR. REIK: But how that will be in the future, we don't know.

DR. FREEMAN: Well, it can't continue this way. Women have the right to be full human beings, as well. And not have to submit to the stereotype of what is masculine and feminine.

DR. REIK: There is of course, something masculine in the most feminine women, and there is something feminine in the most masculine men. For instance, of the great German writers, I would say that Schiller was most masculine. In his plays, the women are feminine but they are also, so to speak, dressed-up men, disguised as women. But Goethe was very feminine; his figures of heroes were really feminine.

DR. FREEMAN: In what sense was he feminine?

DR. REIK: In his life he was feminine. He wanted, for instance, to be more loved.

DR. FREEMAN: But not homosexual?

DR. REIK: No, no. Feminine. There is a difference. I wanted to explain that, and this is a good opportunity. That means, a certain feminity in men is almost a necessary premise for a latent or open homosexuality. Bad? It could be, but there is one out, and that is to go away from the conditions of homosexuality. Let me give a comparison. I learned it from Freud. You want to go to Canada, but you go only to Boston. Now Boston is on the way to Canada, but you don't reach Canada, you go only to Boston. And in this way, a certain feminity while it is one of the premises of homosexuality does not mean that the person is homosexual. Incidentally, to enter sexual relations in order to be loved is feminine. To pretend to love in order to enter sexual relations is masculine. One of the emotional ingredients of femininity would be that a woman would want to be more loved. Not only that she *is* more loved, but also to *hear* that she is more loved.

DR. FREEMAN: And men don't have this?

DR. REIK: No, they don't have that feeling. For men, it's enough to *know*: "My wife loves me" or "My mistress loves me," but they do not need to be told again and again. They need not be reassured *verbally*. That is one of the reasons why it is possible for a gigolo, who says very sweet words and compliments to a woman all the time, to be victorious over a husband, who works all day and provides for the woman. All the husband's thoughts are directed to providing for his woman and not to talking. So one of the differences is that women need the verbal expression—to be told that they are loved. Women are very often won by words. You remember "Othello." Othello wins Desdemona by his telling of his adventures and war experiences, and so on. She listens to him. Why else should it have happened? There was this Venetian nobleman who was much more attractive than the Moor. Otherwise, the successes of men with women would be unexplainable. What attracts them, our beauty? Certainly not.

DR. FREEMAN: In other words, for women words of action speak louder than actions?

DR. REIK: Yes, so to speak.

DR. FREEMAN: But would you also say that women

are sometimes attracted by a component of themselves in a man, and vice versa?

DR. REIK: Yes. For instance, I had one patient who was in love with an overt homosexual. He looked very masculine, but there was something very female about him. Part of the reason she was attracted to him was because he was feminine; he was like her in that way. You could say there was something that attracted her in his homosexuality. Her own homosexuality.

Another patient I had presented a very interesting experience. She had a peculiarity which I didn't understand for a long time. She felt attracted to men who had a physical defect, handicapped. If they limped, or were near-sighted, at least enough to wear glasses. She also had other pathological traits. For instance, she couldn't stay in the same room where there was a cat, which means a bad mother, of course. Then I learned she had a younger brother, and the brother got infantile paralysis. For a long time he had to wear braces, and the mother turned all the attention during this illness, which was in fact very dangerous—he could have died—to this boy, away from the girl. Now, since she was little, this girl wanted to become a boy. And that was one of the reasons, besides penis envy, which made her want to be a boy. She wanted to be loved. And the doctor came to the house with his little bag always, and she thought that at a certain age he would make an operation on her so she could become a boy. Later on, this fantasy of becoming a boy changed its character: she had dark, straight hair, and she thought she would one day wake up with blonde curls. Which, of course, was something she could later on, with all the modern devices, achieve. And she did get blonde curls. She's married now and has two children.

But how deep-reaching the sexual differences between

men and women still remain can easily be concluded from what men get away with and what women get along with.

❧

DR. FREEMAN: How can one tell that one is in love?

DR. REIK: Well, Freud once received a questionnaire asking him to describe the essence of love beyond the realm of sex. And he replied that it was quite impossible for him to fulfill the request. He said: "Really, you ask too much. Up to the present I have not yet found the courage to make any broad statements on the essence of love, and I think that our knowledge is not sufficient." He often quoted a saying: "Love is homesickness." That is correct, of course, for men. Women provide the home.

DR. FREEMAN: Isn't there any basis for deciding?

DR. REIK: For a woman, I would say by the fact that she wants his child.

DR. FREEMAN: And that's the best criterion?

DR. REIK: The best.

DR. FREEMAN: And until you have a feeling like this, you're not in love with a person?

DR. REIK: I would say not—for a woman, we speak now about women.

DR. FREEMAN: And the rest can just be called attraction?

DR. REIK: Well, if you can consider love with such an arbitrary word. Szondi asserts that there are certain laws as valid as the laws of physics and chemistry by which a woman is attracted to a man, to a certain type of man and a man to a certain type of woman. What Helene Deutsch calls a *Schicksal's Neurose*. "*Schicksal*," of course, means "fate." But no woman is attractive to men who doesn't like herself.

But you know, the Jews have a proverb: Love passes time, and time passes love. It means then it goes away, and changes then into a kind of affection. Freud once said to me that a marriage is not secure until the wife becomes maternal to the husband. The woman has it more difficult than the man. As a little girl, she must shift from her first love, mother, to father. But then she can never again find the same satisfaction as she had with mother. Men find it in women, but obviously women not in men. Also, there can be a different situation. For instance, I saw a man here whose wife just had a child with him, and now he feels that he loves her less, he has less sexual desire . . .

DR. FREEMAN: Because of the child?

DR. REIK: Because of the child. We would say the fact that she became a mother reawakens the incest taboo in him. She's a mother, like his mother, no? Unconsciously, of course. Consciously, he has no idea. In other cases, a husband's jealousy of the child, especially if the child is a boy, is there from the beginning.

DR. FREEMAN: Then this is a real paradox, isn't it? For a woman to be in love with a man, and want his child—and then, almost by definition, she takes the risk of losing him.

DR. REIK: Yes, she takes the risk, but he returns to her, of course. He overcomes that, if he is not too neurotic.

DR. FREEMAN: Does the man feel a sense of loss when the woman has an orgasm? Let me explain what I mean. I have a patient who was a ladies' man, an actor, and he had many, many women all the time. The only thing he felt would be the greatest thing he could do would be to cause a woman to have an orgasm. After a while, he met a girl and went to live with her. For a week, he kept saying what a magnificent thing it would be if he could do that for her, because he really loves her, and that's the one thing he wants to do for her. One day he came into the office terribly depressed. He said they had had intercourse the night before, and the girl had an orgasm and she was deliriously happy. And now he feels depressed. He feels that somehow, by having the orgasm, she had stolen something from him.

DR. REIK: To feel something has been stolen from you in sex is a feminine character, as actors in general are. Actors, as far as our experience shows, are slightly schizoid. Otherwise they wouldn't become actors. And judging from what you said, this patient is. Originally, at the time of the Neanderthal Man, or before, the reaction or response of the woman was indifferent. It simply wasn't there. Also, the Neanderthal Man attacked the woman from behind, and it didn't matter to him who the woman was, you know? And she had only the memory of his attack, so to speak. Why did he attack her from behind? Because at this time the sexual drive was not yet so far away from the primitive, from the animals. Anthropologists show us that in the sex life of the most primitive tribes, this position from behind is still preferred. So at that time the response of the woman was one of indifference. It didn't even come into consideration. Then later on, it became so much more personal. And with that the face-to-face position was preferred. And then what finally came was love, which is a late acquisition of mankind. It was not there in the beginning.

DR. FREEMAN: Then the old arrangements for marriages were a cultural parallel to the emotional development? If love came so late in our culture, it didn't really matter.

DR. REIK: I would say "romance" is the better word. Love is such an ambiguous word. To say romance came into human life late is correct.

DR. FREEMAN: Is the sense of deprivation of this man you saw related to the feeling of losing the wife because she became a mother?

DR. REIK: On the contrary. I would say that for most

men—and this is something which women don't know but which they should know—for most men the experience of being a father is something tremendous. Why? It is the final conquest, the mastering of the castration fear. "I am able to produce something! I have reached my father! I can do the same thing he does." That is a victory. The fact that you have a child in your arms which you have produced is for every man the goal, for every man a great experience. For women, of course, too. But for men especially.

DR. FREEMAN: Does it hold for the creative personality like artists, or writers, or actors . . .

DR. REIK: Oh, yes, for them too . . . for Goethe . . .

DR. FREEMAN: Did Goethe have any children?

DR. REIK: Some, yes.

DR. FREEMAN: I didn't know that he was married.

DR. REIK: Yes, late in life. He married a flower girl. We assume that Goethe was impotent until he was forty. Really impotent. And then came his experience in Italy which led him to have a mistress, or several mistresses.

DR. FREEMAN: Perhaps then it would make some men happier to stay home with their children and let the wife, if she is intelligent and has a profession, go out to business.

DR. REIK: Oh, no. That would not do. Let me illustrate. There was in an old *New Yorker* a little sequence of cartoons of the Little King, by Sokoloff. In one of these cartoons, you see the following story: The Little King is a comical king, fat and round. He is invited by the Queen of Sheba to visit her. You see how he crosses the Mediterranean by ship, then you see they are on the other side in Africa. Waiting there are servants with camels and the whole court. Now we see the Little King riding on the camels through the Sahara with his retinue. Then you see he arrives in the palace of the Queen. The Queen leads him around the palace and shows him everything, the throne hall and the banquet hall and her sleeping quarters, and then they go along the corridor and there is a door guarded by slaves with swords. She pushes them aside and opens the door. Inside the room are twenty young men—smoking, playing cards, sleeping—twenty men. And she says: "This is my harem." This is an illustration where women sometimes think there is no such thing as a double standard of morality. That's impossible. You can't do it.

DR. FREEMAN: But why?

DR. REIK: There *is* a double standard.

DR. FREEMAN: Why should there be?

DR. REIK: Well, it seems we come back to the same thing, the biological fact of anatomy. The woman is receptive, she has nothing to attack, generally. Second, her organ is made to receive, not attack. Now biologically, in another sense, you know that animals who get pregnant— let's say a mare—reject every other animal.

DR. FREEMAN: Also the father . . .?

DR. REIK: Often the father, but mostly others. Apes, for instance. Now the thing is the following: It seems that women have fulfilled their function when they are pregnant.

DR. FREEMAN: Once upon a time. But not any more. Maybe it's different now, too.

DR. REIK: No, let us speak only of a woman who is pregnant, rejecting an affair with another man. By the way I have a friend who prefers pregnant women, in the seventh, sixth month.

DR. FREEMAN: Would you consider that strange?

DR. REIK: I would say it's a reversal. He must have been with brothers and sisters. He wants to overcome the incest taboo.

DR. FREEMAN: I have found that one of the problems many women patients have is a kind of ignorance of their own, not responsibilities in sexual activity, but of their rights. Of what they have a right to expect from the man, or from the relationship.

DR. REIK: She can't expect in the first eight days to have an orgasm. But later.

DR. FREEMAN: The question still arises if the education said that the girl is not even supposed to think about it, then she also automatically assumes that she has no rights in the situation once it does arise. But if the education leads to no expectation then this is a kind of pathology.

DR. REIK: Right. Or except if she is pregnant—I know some women patients who reach an orgasm only after they have a pregnancy.

DR. FREEMAN: But up until fairly recently, they had no rights of expectation.

DR. REIK: Yes. In Victorian days, women were not even supposed to have a right to sexual excitement. I remember a woman who said to her husband: "Will you use me this evening?" Use me. Like a necessity. Sexual intercourse, which for a man is a biological necessity, is often for a woman an endurance test. In the opinion of many women, lovemaking should be an act of cult or worship. Otherwise it is in their view a sacrilege. All women wish sexual relations to be legitimate, or at least permanent. Nowadays if a woman is in analysis and she does not eventually reach an orgasm, she should discuss it with her analyst, and complain about it. She has the right to complain. But she must know that she has the right to complain.

Also, a woman who does not reach an orgasm is a danger to a man, to his sense of manhood. There are two excellent criteria for judging when a woman is satisfied, and a man intuitively understands them. The first is when the man had his orgasm, the woman doesn't want him to leave her body. He should stay where he is for a long time. Why? Clearly, because in our depths we are animals. For a man the emission is the end. For a woman it is the beginning. Because the penis inside is now no longer sexual, but symbolically it is the beginning of the embryo. So she wants him to stay. And some women even express it: "Don't leave me." The second excellent criterion is that after sexual intercourse she expresses a great deal of gratitude to that man, as if he has given her a gift, which he has, like the animal, in the same way. But also men know unconsciously if a woman does not reach an orgasm. They know. And then men respond in sexual intercourse, that means that the emission has the feeling of urinating instead of orgasm.

DR. FREEMAN: That reminds me of a patient's dream She was walking on the side of a lake, but the lake was in the city, and where the lake ended the pavement began. She looked down, and in the water was a small fish that looked like a shark cut it in half. In its mouth there was a large p'ece of wood keeping its mouth open, and she thought that there was a hook attached to it. So the shark was not a threat, because it could never close its mouth again, and so wou'd not be dangerous. The next time she looked it was enca°ed in a plastic bag. But it looked too small to be a shark, and too round. Then she got into the water and stood on what seemed like a pogo stick. The stick was moving in the water, and she was standing on the little pedestal, and she was comfortable, But the longer the trip lasted the more worried she became that the stick might tip over and she would fall into the water. Then she decided as long as she is not worried she is safe, and just because it looks like a longer ride than she expected doesn't mean that the stick won't support her. It simply means that if she will have faith and relax and not struggle she will go through the voyage all right. Then she discovered a wall on the left side of her, so she headed for the wall. Coming over the wall was seafoam, and it occurred to her that this was the Adriatic Sea coming over the wall because the water she was riding on was a yellowish color, as though colored with clay.

DR. REIK: But there were no associations?

DR. FREEMAN: No.

DR. REIK: Then you can only guess. That is allowed, of course. What is the sex life of this woman?

DR. FREEMAN: Infrequent. Her husband blames her for the infrequency of the sex life. When they were married she was a virgin, and he holds that against her, he thinks it was stupid.

DR. REIK: What are the contraceptive means?

DR. FREEMAN: She uses a diaphragm.

DR. REIK: Because the dream has something to do with pregnancy. The fish is the male. The spermatozoa perhaps the yellow water. Does she reach an orgasm?

DR. FREEMAN: No, she never has.

DR. REIK: What do you mean she never has? How long do you treat her?

DR. FREEMAN: About half a year. She reaches one when she masturbates.

DR. REIK: Well, you have to analyze that. What is preventing her from reaching it? Does she doubt that this diaphragm is working?

DR. FREEMAN: Not as far as she consciously knows.

DR. REIK: How long did they know each other? Heavy petting?

DR. FREEMAN: Yes.

DR. REIK: That's not good. Freud always said that heavy petting is wrong. He said: "Either you go through with it, or you stay away from each other." Otherwise the woman gets accustomed to the pre-pleasure, without reaching the end pleasure. Not only the orgasm, but psychologically she gets accustomed to this and it would be wrong.

DR. FREEMAN: The patient and her husband used to pet

before they were married. But now if he wants to have intercourse with her, he tells her and that's it.

DR. REIK: Now what the hell does that mean? I tell you something. I have to be very severe with you. That's your fault. You have to educate your patients that women are the educators of men. Not only of little boys, but of men. You know that my wife educated me how to eat. I took a knife which doesn't belong, and so on. Women have to educate men also about sex. Freud said that there was a *Phasen-unterschied*, you know what that is? That means a phase difference between the arousal process in women and in men. In women the process is slower and it goes from tenderness to sex. In men it is the opposite. It sets immediately in with sex, and then to tenderness. That is masculine I would say. Not in bed, but during conversation a woman has to convince the husband that there is a difference. The French, who are so ahead of us in all directions, say: *Un besoin de tendresse, et un besoin de volupté.* "A need of tenderness and a need for voluptuousness." And they have to be together, for the woman, at least. You have to educate men. This prelude need not only be in caressing, it could also be verbal. I think I wrote once in one of my books that women are blessed and cursed with the quality of continuity. That means a man has an argument with his wife at nine o'clock. At eleven he wants to have sexual intercourse. A woman cannot do that. Because before he called her names and so on, and now he wants something sexual from her and she can't find the emotional continuity. You have to make that clear to the patient.

Tell me, did I tell you the story of two patients of mine in Vienna? One of the patients told me of a sexual adventure with a girl. Walking out of my office in Vienna he met this girl, who was also my patient, and he didn't recognize her. And she came into the office and was in a fog, so moved by strong emotion. The affair had happened twenty years before. But she remembered everything about him.

DR. FREEMAN: And he didn't remember?

DR. REIK: Nothing, but nothing. Such sexual adventures don't mean a damn thing to men. It means a roll in the hay and nothing more. I had a patient a few years ago who sat with his wife at the movies and said: "What a beauty Bardot is," and the next time he said it she kicked him. After all she was only on the film. That is too much.

Only a romantic conception might see *La belle dame sans merci* as the woman who coldly refuses the wooing of a man or who does not reciprocate a man's love. *La belle dame sans merci* is rather a woman who refuses to go to bed with the man. Her mercilessness shows in not letting him do as he likes sexually.

That brings me to another point: Why is it that most women in general don't like to be licked in the vagina? Why not? I had a woman patient who let a man do that, and then she said to him, "Pig!" You know? It seems that they feel disgust. It means they feel *he* should be disgusted.

DR. FREEMAN: They feel disgust on his behalf?

DR. REIK: Yes. Menstruation is also part of the reason. Originally there was nothing negative about the menstruation for a woman. On the contrary, there are some women who are most excited during menstruation, sexually excited. An anthropologist wrote that originally men were attracted by the smell of menstruation. So there was a periodicity for women as well as for men. Like when the apes menstruate for instance, the female licks that. Freud was in agreement with that, and he follows that with the question: "Why did it become a negative sign later?" And the answer is, because the man lost his bloodthirst.

DR. FREEMAN: In the Bible, the Jewish *Schulchan Orach* on human relations, it says you're not supposed to have any sexual relations with your wife during her menstrual period.

DR. REIK: Yes, but that's very late in human history. We think about the Neanderthal Man. He was especially affected by the blood smell of the woman.

DR. FREEMAN: Then we can assume that even in Biblical days there must still have been some predilection for it, otherwise why should they specifically forbid it? You don't say, "don't steal" unless people steal.

DR. REIK: One of the reasons for the taboo of the menstruating woman is that men think they will get infected. Because they may think of it as a bleeding wound and they can get infected from it. You know that Nietzsche thought—he eventually became insane you know—he thought women had a razor in their vaginas.

DR. FREEMAN: That sounds psychotic.

DR. REIK: Yes, psychotic. But little boys do think that the vagina is a wound that's left from having lost the penis. That is why when the boy first discovers that there are two sexes he denies it. He says no because it frightens him. I heard of a little boy who after he had seen his sister naked said: "When she grows up she will also get this penis." With that rationalization he avoids a castration fear. When one of my patients was a little boy he called the penis "wee-wee-maker." He had a governess named Ann, and one day he said to his parents: "Ann used to have a wee-wee-maker, but she was naughty, so it was put into the stove." Now the remnants of that were the following: The little boy had a little trumpet, and he blew his trumpet all the time. And this Ann said to him: "Stop that," but he didn't stop. So she said: "If you don't stop that I'll put the trumpet in the stove." Then he must have seen her vagina, and he concluded that she must also have had a penis once, and it was taken away in the same way she had threatened to do to his trumpet.

DR. FREEMAN: What about the theory that women are supposed to be so much more masochistic than men?

DR. REIK: In general. But not in particular. And not on this point. How many female martyrs were there?

DR. FREEMAN: All I can think of is Saint Joan.

DR. REIK: She was not even a martyr. The early Christian martyrs. Thousands and thousands of men are thrown to the lions.

DR. FREEMAN: And they didn't throw the women?

DR. REIK: No.

DR. FREEMAN: Maybe because they became slaves?

DR. REIK: No. Because women have not this fanaticism of men.

DR. FREEMAN: And yet you say that women are more religious than men.

DR. REIK: I would say that superstitiousness is one of the universal traits of women. Women are less rebellious in religion. They are much less atheists than men. Show me many women who are atheists. They are not. Heine said: "A woman without religion is like a flower without a scent." If a woman has not religion she usually has superstition at least, which is substitute religion.

DR. FREEMAN: The church is the mother church.

DR. REIK: This is quite different. Anatole France tells the story: a girl in Provence goes to the chapel and kneels down before the Holy Virgin and says: "You who have conceived without sinning, give me the grace to sin without conceiving." The relationship to the mother and father is different. Anatole France also tells that a man, a Parisian aristocrat, sees a woman kneel down before the altar and observes that she is that pious because the position is becoming—to her breasts and her figure.

DR. FREEMAN: Then would you say that women do more things for the sake of appearances. . . .

DR. REIK: Yes. They are always under observation. A

woman entering a room, on a social occasion, cocktail party, social gathering, has a feeling everybody looks her over, a man not. And it is generally true, that women are looked at. Men are looked at too, but they don't experience it.

DR. FREEMAN: And men are not concerned about what impression they make?

DR. REIK: Much less, much less.

DR. FREEMAN: Then the more concerned they are, the greater the feminine component?

DR. REIK: The more they are, the more feminine they are, right. Also the more they are aware of the room, or furnishings.

DR. FREEMAN: You mean of their surroundings?

DR. REIK: Yes. When you hear a man who is very much concerned about the drapes, the curtains and the colors, you would say he is very feminine. In reality it should be a woman who would notice such things. I personally don't give a damn about what a room looks like.

DR. FREEMAN: So, then for instance if a man is an interior decorator you would say he was inclined to be a homosexual.

DR. REIK: Inclined, yes. Also, oversensitiveness to damaging of material is a feminine trait. It is a displacement to outside objects. For instance when a leather bag gets scratched.

DR. FREEMAN: Well, then, what about the difference between the feelings that a man has for someone else's sensibilities and the feelings a woman has—in other words, for being tactful or tactless.

DR. REIK: Men are less.

DR. FREEMAN: You mean men are less concerned with how they make people feel?

DR. REIK: Right, much less concerned. Think for instance that a woman almost never forgets birthdays and especially the anniversary of her marriage. Men have to be reminded, in general they are forgetful about this.

On the other hand men cannot say catty things. A woman told of one woman coming to visit another and commenting on her new carpet. She said: "I always say that there is nothing like a new carpet to bring together old lived-in furniture." That is, of course, a negative thing in the compliment. Or: "Bessie, you are always so well-groomed and well taken care of, I wonder how old you have to become until you take such good care of yourself."

DR. FREEMAN: In other words, the attack is not direct.

DR. REIK: Never direct. Only in great, unusual upheaval. When I was in Vienna, there was a famous story. Two women met each other in one of the best dress shops. One was Jeritza, the famous soprano in the Vienna opera, I forgot who the other woman was. But they got into each other's hair, really, because they each had the same dress. By accident. The one dress came from Paris, and the other was made in Vienna after the Paris model. Can you imagine two men getting into a fight because they have the same suit? Contrast a haberdasher who says to a man in London: "Take this hat, sir. All the men in the city are wearing it." On the other hand to a woman in a hat store, the saleswoman will say: "Madam, take this hat, no other woman is wearing it."

DR. FREEMAN: In other words the sense of individualization is stronger in women?

DR. REIK: Yes. They want to be different.

DR. FREEMAN: Why is that?

DR. REIK: That goes very deep. It goes into the sexual sphere. Women are much more alike than men are. All women go through menstruation, childbirth, menopause, *climakterium*. Men not. So biologically women are much more alike than men.

DR. FREEMAN: Then women's need to be different from each other is a social manifestation of the biological condition?

DR. REIK: Of a deeper biological difference.

DR. FREEMAN: But there is a contradiction inherent in this. If the assumption is that all women are the same, then why do men want to have experiences with more than one woman?

DR. REIK: They find out much later that biologically all women are the same. Not at first. The attraction of the woman has something to do with the secret location of the genitals. This is the deep secret they are looking for.

DR. FREEMAN: The attraction is psychological rather than biological. Then women try to differentiate themselves from other women so that men will respond as though they were in fact different?

DR. REIK: Yes, "as though." That's right. Even though a man would always say: "What can I find, I find the same genital there, as with any other woman." You know in America they have a saying in the Marines: "Cover her head with the stars and stripes and it is the same." Meaning one woman is like another. But still it doesn't make any difference, they keep looking. The best continuation of this train of thought would be dress. Is a woman interested in the kind of trousers a man has? What he wears below the waist? No, not much. But a man is interested in what a woman wears. Her stockings, her shoes, and so on. Because he searches for the genital. He is always in search of the genital, which is invisible.

DR. FREEMAN: That must have been a very interesting phenomenon in ancient Greece, where a woman wore diaphanous clothes.

DR. REIK: Not so.

DR. FREEMAN: I just read, I forgot where, that for a while there was a complaint in ancient Greece about the way women dressed, not on moral grounds, but because if they dress in these clothes for everyone to see on the street, then what is left for the husband?

DR. REIK: But they were wrong, because one can never see the woman's genitals, however transparent the clothes. They are located in such a way that you cannot see them.

DR. FREEMAN: Is there a possibility then, that excessive promiscuity on the part of a man . . .

DR. REIK: Excessive? There is no excessive. A man could have a hundred women in a year, if he is young. But sometimes a hundred girls are not as dangerous as one. What did Freud say? That the relationship between men and women is governed by a strange arithmetic: many are too little and one is too much.

DR. FREEMAN: In other words you are saying man is continually in search for the genitals. And that is all it consists of?

DR. REIK: Yes. That is, of course, displaced to the face, the figure, consciously.

DR. FREEMAN: In other words, if someone says: "I don't care about women's legs, I just care about faces," that is displacement upward?

DR. REIK: Yes.

DR. FREEMAN: Poor men. I suppose we'll have to do something to broaden their horizon.

DR. REIK: Yes, good. But there still seems to be so much confusion between love and sex. Look here, sex is a biological urge, a chemical situation, an organic tension that a person needs to rid himself of. It is a quest for physical satisfaction and concerns the choice of a body, or even one's own. It is, in general, indiscriminate. One desires the sex object only during the sex act—and someone who is sexually satisfied can still feel love starved, and very often depressed, even after intercourse. Love on the other hand is an emotional craving. There is a need to escape from

one's own inadequacy, and so there is a creation of individual imagination and preference. Love concerns the
choice of a particular individual personality, it is directed
at that specific personality. And the person remains continually the object of one's tenderness and caring. One
can never be indifferent to that person even after one is
sexually satisfied.

A normal attitude and expression in one's love life is
possible only if the sexual impulses and the tender caring
impulses meet in the same person. The problem arises
when there is a split between one's feelings of sexuality and
one's tenderness and liking for the person. Love removes
fear. It is impossible to love someone you are afraid of and
vice versa. To love satisfies a desire to give tenderness, to
belong to someone. It is to feel humble towards the person
one loves. A blow to one's self-confidence can be felt as a
mortal pain if that blow is dealt by someone we love. After
all, one of the emotions that governs our lives is the need
to be loved. I wrote a book by that title where I discuss
this.

DR. FREEMAN: What about the differences of guilt feelings in men and women?

DR. REIK: Women have very little sense of guilt. Sachs
pointed that out very early, that women have a much
weaker super-ego than men. That means it is connected
with convention, with what will people say and so on. For
a man, a cop is the personification of law, for a woman, he
is a man in uniform. Nothing else.

DR. FREEMAN: And the kinds of things women feel
guilty about are not the same as men?

DR. REIK: No. For example, women have very little
sense of guilt about sexuality. And in general they feel
less guilt.

DR. FREEMAN: I think in general they have less to feel guilty about because they are not so violent.

DR. REIK: Yes, biologically women don't have the same violent tendencies.

DR. FREEMAN: And therefore biologically the superego is less developed?

DR. REIK: Yes, less developed, except very masculine women. Lady Macbeth has that. Lady Macbeth in general has very little feminine—she is much more masculine. First, she has murderous tendencies although she doesn't murder. Second, she is not superstitious. And all women are superstitious. There is no exception. And third, she never asked Macbeth what the witches were wearing. She never asked that.

DR. FREEMAN: There is a paradox in all that. There are more men criminals than women. Could it be that women are the cultural super-ego?

❦

DR. REIK: Women are not afraid of men. But men are afraid of women.

DR. FREEMAN: I disagree.

DR. REIK: Well, perhaps, you're right—we men think we are the only ones who are afraid.

JEWISHNESS

DR. REIK: By the way, I had a strong memory which I wanted to tell you about. In a letter Freud wrote to Sandor Ferenczi, he says ". . . that assurance that the children will be provided for, which, for a Jewish father, is a matter of life and death."

DR. FREEMAN: Is that the Jewish father's own kind of immortality?

DR. REIK: It seems so, yes, if he thinks of such immortality. Freud didn't believe much in immortality. But it's nice: " . . . with a Jewish father it is a matter of life and death." By the way, the other day, I heard a Jewish proverb: "A Jew, in order to secure an education for his children, invents a sky."

DR. FREEMAN: Very nice. How would you explain why this is important to a Jewish father?

DR. REIK: The father's responsibility in the Jewish family is different from the father's in non-Jewish families. He feels it more strongly.

155

DR. FREEMAN: Does a Jewish father resent it when his son becomes better than he?

DR. REIK: On the contrary, he enjoys it. The Jews would say, "My son, the doctor" with greater pride. Whereas a non-Jew would say: "What is good enough for me is good enough for him." This is a basic kind of difference towards the son.

DR. FREEMAN: Why is there that difference?

DR. REIK: Because in Jewish families the belongingness is not horizontal, but vertical—it goes through generations. The Ten Commandments say: "Honor your father and mother."

DR. FREEMAN: "so thy days may be long. . . ."

DR. REIK: ". . . so that you live on the land which I have given you." And that does not mean that *you* personally should live in the Promised Land, but the tribe should. That is an important difference. It does not mean personal immortality; it means immortality for the tribe.

DR. FREEMAN: Then in a sense, what happens is that the honor for mother and father . . .

DR. REIK: . . . becomes the roots for the Jew, instead of the country in which he lives. Because he has had no country in which he lived more than four generations. And this attitude is then transferred from the parents to each country in which they live.

DR. FREEMAN: Then there is a reciprocal kind of relationship in this between father and son—honor for the one and pride in the accomplishment of the other. But perhaps there really is a paradox here, an ambivalence. If the father is proud of his sons for accomplishing more, is there some resentment at the same time?

DR. REIK: Unconsciously. Consciously, he enjoys that . . .

DR. FREEMAN: And the non-Jewish father who says: "It

was good enough for my father—or for me—it's good enough for my sons . . ."

DR. REIK: My father, or our fathers . . .

DR. FREEMAN: But doesn't that in some way affect the dynamics of the father-son relationship?

DR. REIK: Certainly it does. Because also in the case of the Fifth Commandment—it does not say you should *love* your father and mother. It says you should *honor* them— there's a great difference. And they do that, Jewish children honor them.

DR. FREEMAN: Then love is only in connection with God.

DR. REIK: Love cannot be commanded, cannot be ordered. You cannot order someone: Love me!

DR. FREEMAN: Then the Old Testament really understands human nature—because the Ten Commandments are concerned with those matters which can be obeyed if they are commanded.

DR. REIK: Yes.

DR. FREEMAN: But some of the Christian commandments by definition cannot be obeyed, no matter how much one might want to.

DR. REIK: Right. They are commanded to love.

DR. FREEMAN: So that, in a sense, the Jewish religion makes a commandment of that which can be obeyed and rationally performed. It is subject to the conscious will of the person.

DR. REIK: Right. Because you can always show your father honor, you can perform your duty. So such commandments do not really affect the emotional life of the Jew. And yet he has guideposts.

DR. FREEMAN: The guideposts are rational—

DR. REIK: Yes, rational, not irrational.

Dr. Freeman: But the manifestations, the way in which you execute the guideposts—they are emotional.

Dr. Reik: Yes, good. But on the other hand, the commandments could be only a certain tool, because honoring your father and mother means to show them honor, to behave in a certain way. I read the other day, stories from England about nineteenth century British Jews. The father of the family dies, and two or three days later the son sits down in his chair. The mother gets very upset, and she chases him out: "You cannot sit in *that* chair"—the father's chair, you know?

Dr. Freeman: But he can sit in a better chair.

Dr. Reik: Yes. Or he can keep standing, or complain, or be angry and unpleasant. And then his mother will either be upset with him or angry in return, or punish him.

Dr. Freeman: So that the results are, that if you behave in a certain way, you stimulate the environment to behave back in a certain way.

Dr. Reik: Yes, and that then depends upon who is the environment and what do they feel about you. And if the Oedipal situation has not been resolved, then the effect is often negative.

Dr. Freeman: Do you think that bigotry or the tendency to bigotry is in some ways related to a loveless childhood?

Dr. Reik: Bigotry? I would say it is connected to what you learn as a child from your surroundings.

Dr. Freeman: Do you think that a child of a non-loving mother can also be bigoted simply because she hates?

Dr. Reik: I think so. I have at the moment one patient who really is an anti-Semite. He cannot rid himself of anti-Semitism entirely, even though he is attracted to

Jewish men and women both. And it has to do with the fact that his father was anti-Semitic, his mother, too. He was brought up like that. And he recognizes, so to speak, only those traits in Jews which are ostentatious. It is interesting, too, that whenever an anti-Semite talks, he always speaks of the Jews *all over the world*, as though it wasn't just the one Jew in his country. It's always the international Jew—the cosmopolitan Jew.

DR. FREEMAN: It's the sense that the Jew is the same Jew in London as he is in Russia.

DR. REIK: Yes, which he isn't, strangely enough.

Erika, I have an idea. Let's write a book together about the Jews. Don't look so surprised. I know I said I wasn't going to write any more. But this one we could do together very well, too. I want to call it "The Unreachables," because everybody seems to feel that somehow Jews are strange and unreachable.

DR. FREEMAN: That's a lovely idea. But I have the feeling that we don't really agree about the Jews.

DR. REIK: Well, I think that Jews have a repetition compulsion. They were in their mother country and they were taken out of it by force and brought into new countries. Like Babylon. And thereafter they have repeated their history according to the definition of repetition compulsion—which means that an individual reproduces and re-enacts the traumatic event, instead of only remembering it and learning the lesson from it. So the Jews come to certain countries, are even invited to come, as they were in Poland, for instance, and then make their contributions in science and medicine and literature and so on, and are then persecuted and thrown out by the host country.

DR. FREEMAN: It seems to me the other way around. It is gentiles who have the repetition compulsion. They are the ones who are drawn to them, use them, and then persecute them or insist that they stop being Jews. The first real organized anti-Semitic persecutions were by Christians. The ancients were, at worst, ambivalent towards them.

DR. REIK: That's an interesting point. Nevertheless the repetitive core is the recurring migrations of the Jews. In one of her books, George Eliot—incidentally Freud thought she had remarkable insights—puts the following sentence into the mouth of one of the Jewish characters —in *Daniel Deronda*, I think—"Our people wandered before they were driven out." Also don't forget that in their wanderings the Jews were not violent. They never had an Attila the Hun. Imagine when a large migration of Jews came to this country, if someone were to say they are a dangerous group because they are violent, everyone would laugh. And rightly so. Because the Jews are a people of the book and of the family. They laugh at the Jew because he sits and studies. Jews don't even hunt animals for sport. Even fishing for sport is not something that is part of their culture. How many Jewish people do you know who go fishing on weekends for recreation? So far the one or two that I know of are all assimilated and trying to belong to another group. So you can imagine how the Nazis or anyone who prefers violence have to hate the Jews. And of course by projection they call the Jews inferior.

DR. FREEMAN: Do you think part of the Jewish repetition compulsion is that they put themselves at the service of people who then turn their violent impulses back upon the Jews?

DR. REIK: Yes. That too is a part of it. And I'll tell you something else. I don't think a country can afford not to have any Jews. Look what happened in Spain since the Inquisition. Even the Germans invited Jews back, and look at the cultural life in Vienna. Even in America, consider their contributions to art and literature and music. It is ironic that the Viennese who don't like Jews at all invited Leonard Bernstein to conduct there. But they love music. So they knew what they were doing.

DR. FREEMAN: Their love of culture didn't exactly stop them from their anti-Semitism and persecuting their Jews during the Nazi time.

DR. REIK: It is interesting about the Viennese. They have such a cosmopolitan city and yet they are in many ways so provincial. But then don't forget that whenever a country becomes irrational, that is, when they don't have any respect for reason or human life, one of the first things that happens in their emotional life is that they become anti-Semitic.

DR. FREEMAN: That even happens to irrational young Jews.

DR. REIK: That is, of course, self-hatred. Unconscious, of course. And they usually take the side against Jews with the rationalization that it is more human, or enlightened when often all it really is, is a rejection of their own parents.

❧

DR. FREEMAN: Is there a difference in approach in psychoanalysis between Jews and non-Jews.

DR. REIK: No, I don't think so.

DR. FREEMAN: Someone was speaking about the difference between psychiatrist and psychoanalysts and said that a great preponderance of psychoanalysts among the psychiatrists were Jewish.

DR. REIK: That is what Menninger said. In a chapter in one of his books he spoke of the "Jewish genius for psychoanalysis" and he even points that out.

DR. FREEMAN: But Menninger is not Jewish.

DR. REIK: No, certainly not. You remember I mentioned that when Jung was the editor of the psychological journal during the Nazi days, he tried to make the distinction and simply said that there was Gentile psychology, and then there was Jewish psychology which is psychoanalysis. That, of course, is not true. It was only an expression of his personal anti-Semitism.

DR. FREEMAN: I think the reason for the seemingly Jewish talent for psychoanalysis is that we are all basically Talmudists.

DR. REIK: Yes, that's good. After all, don't we question everything?

DR. FREEMAN: How do you explain the fact that there are so many anti-Semites who will nevertheless come to the Jewish analyst.

DR. REIK: During the history of the Jews, the Jews always played a great role as psychiatrists, as physicians, even in Spain.

By the way, do you know of Torquemada?

DR. FREEMAN: The chief of the Spanish Inquisition?

DR. REIK: Yes. After all is said and done, he was just another bloody sadist.

CREATIVE PEOPLE

DR. FREEMAN: What is necessary for creativity?

DR. REIK: Perhaps isolation, psychologically. And yet not total isolation. Because you address yourself to an audience when you create, in your fantasy you address yourself to someone. And writers and painters, for instance, they infect each other. At first they sit around and talk, and then they have to go away to put it together. Van Gogh to Arles, Gauguin to the South Seas, Pissarro home. But the infection came first from a mutual kind of talent, a kind of interaction. Then they go away and become selective, where no one can answer back.

DR. FREEMAN: And then the artist addresses himself to the one person who gave him the idea—himself or someone else—and answers in his own way, whether it be poetry or painting. So I think creativity has to be both the result of interaction and the result of some inner drive. It's like plugging into an electric socket—but you have to have an organism that can light up. And many don't. I

163

think that one is impossible without the other. The artist expresses himself—and if he is really an artist, then in the act of expressing himself he is also expressing everyone else. If not . . .

DR. REIK: Then he is not an artist. But to do the actual work he must be alone. What is that nonsense they speak about now—"creative upholstery," and such?

Jones said that music is connected with anality. That means to say it is the enjoyment of the noises which are originally in one's own body. Freud originally thought that gifts are biological, inherited. Not necessarily. I would say that actors have stronger possibilities to be homosexuals than people in general. And the women who are actresses are more masculine.

DR. FREEMAN: It seems to me that actors suffer from a kind of lack of identity.

DR. REIK: That is right. One would say they are all schizoid.

DR. FREEMAN: I should think they would have to be, because they have to be someone else all the time. So that the chances are that the male actor would be more likely to be homosexual and the female actress would be more likely to be homosexual as well.

But why is that? An actor exhibits himself, and presenting oneself to be admired is a feminine trait. So if an actress exhibits herself to be admired isn't that a feminine thing to do?

DR. REIK: No, I wouldn't say that. It would be a feminine thing if she would disguise that desire.

DR. FREEMAN: In other words, if she wanted to be an actress and pretended she didn't.

DR. REIK: I would say that is more feminine. A woman need not be an actress professionally, because she is one in life.

DR. FREEMAN: Would that mean women are a little more schizoid than men, in any case?

DR. REIK: I wouldn't go that far. Actors as a profession are more so.

DR. FREEMAN: But don't women tend to play parts?

DR. REIK: Yes, they play parts, that's correct.

DR. FREEMAN: Do you think that possibly a writing block in women, assuming for a moment that it is sexually linked, that it could be part of the unwillingness to expose?

DR. REIK: Yes, it could be. But there is something else to that. Men have much more hostility, aggressiveness, than women. So that their reactions, their inhibitions, are the greater. That means if there were aggressiveness or violence in their nature—which it is clear that there is—then they would react much more to guilt feelings, they would think something violent, murderous wishes, and so on. Women are more tolerant. Women have a milder super-ego.

DR. FREEMAN: Milder super-ego?

DR. REIK: Much milder, much milder. For a man this cop there on the corner is a personification of the law. Even for the gangster who shoots him. The cop is called "the law" in the gangsters' language sometimes. But for a woman this cop is just a uniformed man—with whom she could talk, whom she could convince that the car, that she didn't drive it in this way, and so on.

DR. FREEMAN: In other words she sees him as a person, not a symbol?

DR. REIK: She has not this terrible respect. Women also have a milder super-ego with regard to orthography —if they make a mistake in writing, it doesn't matter so much.

DR. FREEMAN: Then are you saying that women who do have such a highly developed super-ego and have the same kinds of blocks, they have a larger aggressiveness, they are more masculine?

DR. REIK: Yes, they are more masculine.

DR. FREEMAN: So that a writing block is almost a masculine manifestation for a woman?

DR. REIK: But not necessarily. I would say writing has a special meaning. Writing, as Freud told us at the end of his life, is connected with urinating, which physiologically is easier for a woman—they have a wider bladder.

DR. FREEMAN: But that still would mean that a writing block in a woman when it wasn't the fear of exposure, for instance, would be a masculine component.

DR. REIK: Yes, good. In general, you could say that. But what the hell, writing! The great task of a woman is to bring a child into the world. Only men are foolish enough—they are so vain they think that they are the fulfillment of a woman's life. That's not true. The man is not the fulfillment, the baby is. She has done something which no man would be able to, she brought a child into the world.

That means that for the man their work is, so to speak, a second best. For a woman it also would be second best, because the first is the baby. While we are thinking in either terms, in the men's terms, for instance, there are certain men who are envious of women and who say: "Well, I have my work. I can write, I can show a book instead of a baby." And they call it that: "It's my baby" is the slang.

DR. FREEMAN: Is it possible that the women who are always being urged to produce—I don't mean babies, but work or in literature—but can't. . . .

DR. REIK: Well, they must have a block with regard to babies.

DR. FREEMAN: Or if they find it difficult to produce, then perhaps they don't want to settle for second best.

In other words, if the urging comes from the outside, people say: "You have so much talent, and you can do this and this, why don't you write?" And then she blocks.

DR. REIK: She should have a baby.

DR. FREEMAN: And then she will write?

DR. REIK: Sometimes, yes.

Also, it is quite clear there is the following perspective: the creative life of the woman lasts only a short time with regard to children. It is marked by the menopause. What does she do then? The children grow up, what does she do with her life? She should have something to fall back to.

DR. REIK: I wanted to talk about people who are creative with comedy. In connection with that, I was with some other analysts, and one analyst said something about another analyst. He was trying to be funny, but it was an insult to the other analyst. I think it is bad taste for someone in an analyst's position to say that another analyst is "off his rocker"—to sacrifice everything for one laugh. Also when he introduced that Hungarian analyst and said: "It is not enough to be Hungarian. One must also have talent." That is bad taste.

DR. FREEMAN: That reminds me, in America most of the comedians are Jews.

DR. REIK: Yes, good. But that was not always so. You have that book of mine on wit. There I point out that Jewish jokes were originally a tribal kind of amusement, only among Jews. Jews told other Jews stories.

DR. FREEMAN: Well, the thing that reminded me is what you said about a man who sacrifices everything for one laugh. Is this the kind of phenomenon that goes on in comedians?

DR. REIK: Yes.

DR. FREEMAN: What do they get from this?

DR. REIK: They sacrifice their dignity. For Jews, it is funny if they tell it to other Jews. But if they tell it to gentiles, the gentiles misunderstand that. I pointed that out in one of my books, too.

DR. FREEMAN: But about comedians in general?

DR. REIK: There must be a self-degradation.

DR. FREEMAN: A kind of masochism.

DR. REIK: Right. But on the other hand it can also be sadism if he attacks other people.

There is a wonderful story I read that comedians in France tell about De Gaulle. A man comes to De Gaulle after the elections and says: "My God, you were again victorious!" And De Gaulle says: "*Merci bien*. But call me '*Mon general*.' "

DR. FREEMAN: What are the kinds of feelings that a comedian experiences when he goes after laughter?

DR. REIK: Masochism, in general. A kind of exhibitionism which is masochistic. And you know there is a rarity of female comediennes. First of all, they are not so masochistic. Second, they are not so anxious to make a spectacle of themselves in this masochistic way.

Although it is much better to women, the stage. They have a natural kind of exhibitionism, no? Which is not in men.

DR. FREEMAN: Then you would consider exhibitionism a feminine trait?

DR. REIK: Certainly. Their figure, their beauty, their charm.

DR. FREEMAN: And yet in effect—this was something else I noticed with actors—once they can work again, they have a sense of seducing the audience. So that in that sense the women become masculine again. They seduce the audience, not they by the audience.

DR. REIK: Yes, they tempt, so to speak, the audience. Well, that is an actor.

DR. FREEMAN: When actors come into therapy, they come as ten different people. And for the first few months, every day you're treating somebody different.

DR. REIK: All actors that I have known are schizoid. You know the French even speak of a *schizoïde supérieur*. There can be genius among these actors.

DR. FREEMAN: And this panic most of them seem to have about marriage. It seems to be a more severe panic than most men have before they marry. What is the cause of that?

DR. REIK: They don't want to be fenced in.

DR. FREEMAN: Might it not also be that if they are married the threat is too close. There is a woman constantly present.

DR. REIK: Yes, watching. And perhaps they are afraid of having their feminine attributes discovered.

DR. FREEMAN: And the women who go on the stage, that is an expression of their masculinity. Even though in both cases, in men and in women, it is exhibitionism?

DR. REIK: Yes. But they are opposite kinds. A woman is naturally exhibitionistic and seductive. But when she goes on the stage she is going beyond that and is using her masculine component—to seduce the audience and so on. If that drive is too strong, then she may be homosexual. But it need not be. Everyone has the opposite—masculinity and femininity—in them; it's natural. Men do not have this kind of exhibitionism. So if a man goes on the stage to be admired and so on, he is also going beyond the masculine component and using his feminine component. That too is natural in him. But if it goes too far, then he can be homosexual. But you know a great deal about actors and creative people in general, you should do your own book on that. I shall write you an introduction to that, as I shall also write you an introduction to your book of aphorisms.

I don't know whether I told you about Yvette Guilbert?
Yvette Guilbert was a great diseuse and she was a friend
of Freud, she and her husband. She was a great artist.
She spoke sitting down, poems. She was everything from
a vagabond, to a prostitute, or a flirting woman, or a
grandmother—everybody. And when she spoke you saw
these people. There is one wonderful poem which is still
in my ear. Freud never missed an opportunity to go to
hear her when she was in Vienna. I once went with him.
They exchanged many letters. One ballad was, a boy had
an affair with a girl. And the girl wanted only to play
with him, so she said to him: "Go and get me the heart
of your mother for my dog." And the boy ran and killed
his mother and tore out her heart and ran back to this
mistress. And while he ran so much, he stumbled and fell
down. And the heart rolled in the dust, and the heart said:
"*T'es-tu fait mal, mon enfant?*" "Did you hurt yourself,
my child?"

In a letter Yvette Guilbert wrote to Freud, she told
about the book she was writing, *Les Chansons de ma Vie*,
—The Songs of My Life. In this book, she wanted to explain her theory that an artist is expanding his personality
so that he can act like somebody entirely strange, like
Richard the Third, or Hamlet, or someone else. Freud
said in his answer to her that he had very few experiences
with actors, but what he can guess is that her theory is
not correct. That an actor is a person who lives out
potentialities within him which are not lived out in life.
And so she asked him: "How can I then play so many
roles?" And he said: "That shows only that potentially
you are a very rich personality. That you have all these
potentialities as destinies in you, and need not choose. You
can act them all out." In a later letter, which I think he
wrote to her husband, he explained that the only other
actor he liked was Charlie Chaplin. And Charlie Chaplin

grew up in the poorest East end of London. And he always plays the same role. Neglected, dumb, *nebbish*. And so Freud says those are his memories of his childhood, which he brings out again and again. So to speak, mastering these experiences of the early childhood.

DR. FREEMAN: What was the creative life of Vienna like?

DR. REIK: Vienna was a strange city, at least when I was there. I remember that Mahler, Gustav Mahler, complained about how long it was before he first heard that Schnitzler was enthusiastic about his Sixth Symphony. Mahler always said what a terrible thing that is, that we live in a city where no one knows the other person. It is not like here in New York where literary people meet each other. They were separate.

Gustav Mahler, whom I worship . . . did I tell you about that?

DR. FREEMAN: No.

DR. REIK: I remember that once I walked on the Ringstrasse. It was late evening. As I walked and whistled, I knew that Mahler was walking behind me. I must have been eighteen. And suddenly he walked beside me and asked: "What are you whistling there?" And I said: "The Andante of your Second Symphony." He said: "Good, good," and shook my hand and ran off.

DR. FREEMAN: Had you met him by then?

DR. REIK: No, never. Only this one time.

The strange thing was that when I was about nineteen, I fell in love with Mahler's wife. She was old enough to be my mother. She was a very impressive figure, a kind of Brünnhilde sort, you know. I saw her at the opera, at concerts. She was gentile, of course, and I fell in love with her. In reality I was in love with him, with Mahler, but I had shifted that, displaced it, to her. And then I met her in Amsterdam, and I said: "Oh God! She could have been my grandmother, not my mother."

DR. FREEMAN: You had only seen her, you had never met her?

DR. REIK: No, later on I met her.

DR. FREEMAN: How did you meet her finally?

DR. REIK: She invited me. She knew who I was, of course. There was a performance of the Fourth Symphony, and she was in a box. When I came in, there was a long parquette, and she waved at me I should come up. And I sat beside her. Her husband was dead at the time, he died in 1911. It was a triumph for me unconsciously—it was a renewal of the victories of overcoming incest, because I sat with her, and he was dead, and together we heard the Fourth Symphony. And later on when she had married Franz Werfel, she invited me there to Breitenstein, also on Semmering. Mahler himself had built a cottage there. Franz Werfel was at this time in great rebellion against psychoanalysis and Freud, and he was shifting to Catholicism more and more.

DR. FREEMAN: Didn't she know Bruno Walter, also?

DR. REIK: Yes.

DR. FREEMAN: Did she ever marry him?

DR. REIK: Oh no, she was not in love with him. Someone else was in love with her, this . . . what's his name, this painter . . . ?

DR. FREEMAN: Kokoschka. She must have been a remarkable woman.

DR. REIK: Oh, she was, she was. She wanted to compose herself, but gave it up later on.

DR. FREEMAN: And Mahler was much older than she.

DR. REIK: Oh, certainly he was much older—about twenty years. I told you, didn't I, that he was in analysis with Freud?

DR. FREEMAN: Yes. Speaking of that, there's a common fear among people in the arts—painters, writers, musicians, and so on—that if they go into analysis they will lose their creativity.

DR. REIK: Yes, that is a fear. Freud wrote in one of his letters that when there is a real talent, it will only be deepened by analysis. But if there's a minimal talent there, then it will, of course, destroy itself.

PATIENTS

DR. FREEMAN: This is a young actor in his mid-twenties, not married. All his brothers are married. He was referred to me by a colleague, because he complained that the analyst was treating him according to the book, and he didn't want to be treated according to the book.

DR. REIK: Yes, he wanted to be treated individually.

DR. FREEMAN: Then he came to see me and we discussed first of all what his objection was to the other analyst, because he had only seen him twice, and I didn't know whether it was resistance to analysis in general or some negative feeling towards this man. It turns out that there was some realistic objection. But in any case he decided he would rather come to me. Now, for about one month he never saw the other analyst, but he never uncommitted himself to him, either. In other words, he always made an appointment with the other analyst, and the day before every appointment he would cancel it. When he finally told me about this, I told him that he would have to make a choice, because it wasn't fair to the other analyst. I discussed the possibility with him that he didn't want to give up his audience. He had said that the other analyst was a great audience, whereas with me he felt that he was talking to another actor, and he couldn't pretend anything because I'd know when it was acting technique and when not.

For about another month after that he was extremely verbal. He talked freely about his childhood, and about his girlfriend. One day he told me that he was going to be married but that it was a secret. He said they were on the way to City Hall to get a marriage license, but then he realized that he would be late for his appointment with me. So they gave the taxi driver my address. Now, this is a patient who has always been late, almost congenitally.

DR. REIK: With you, too?

DR. FREEMAN: Yes. He always came ten minutes late for his sessions, until he cancelled the other analyst for good. After that he came on time.

DR. REIK: The connection was that he had decided to stay with you and now was committed.

DR. FREEMAN: Yes. About two sessions ago he suddenly stopped talking. He came in and said: "I'm not going to talk today. I don't think I can have a session." I asked him what happened and he said: "I didn't do what I set out to do. I set out to get the marriage license and didn't get it. If I set out to do something I must finish it. And I didn't finish that, so I'm very upset with myself." I suggested the possibility that he was angry with me, that he considered it my fault that he hadn't finished what he started. He said, no, no if that were the case he'd let me know about it. And then for a good fifteen minutes he said nothing else.

Then he said: "I'm still mad from last time, because I met another patient of yours." That was a fellow actor and they had been in a play together. The other actor was better known then than this one. He said: "I think you're giving him preferential treatment and you are not supposed to." I asked him what made him think I was giving the other one preferential treatment. "Well," he answered, "He doesn't always come after me. Sometimes he isn't there. I think the reason he isn't here is because he is in rehearsal and therefore, for his convenience you gave him another time. And I'm not going to talk anymore today. I'm not having a session. So what do I do now?" So I said: "If you don't want to talk you don't have to talk. It's your session. But this too is one way of having a session. There is no law that says you must talk every minute of the hour." Well, he said he thought that was what he was mad about, but he wasn't going to talk anymore. Finished. And he didn't speak for the rest of the hour.

DR. REIK: You cannot do that. You cannot let him.

DR. FREEMAN: No, I mean voluntarily. He spoke, but only in response to my questions. I felt that in a sense he was manipulating me—to make me talk by asking him questions.

DR. REIK: But it means that he keeps something secret. Can you guess what his secret is?

DR. FREEMAN: What?

DR. REIK: He is in love with you. Don't laugh, Erika. That's clear. Shall the man tell you that? Now, look, a guy who goes out to marry and remembers he has a session with you and returns, says: "I prefer you." That's quite clear.

DR. FREEMAN: I didn't know why they suddenly decided to get married. They had been living together for two years.

DR. REIK: Now, this is nothing against the girl, but it is something for you.

DR. FREEMAN: Well, I expected some kind of transference, but not this kind.

DR. REIK: Does he know you are married?

DR. FREEMAN: Yes.

DR. REIK: Certainly. So he displaces his jealousy to this other actor.

DR. FREEMAN: I asked him for a dream, then. When he first began analysis he said: "I'm very good with dreams. I always remember them." But in the beginning I felt he would try to manipulate the situation by always telling dreams—a kind of resistance. So I didn't ask about dreams, but if he'd mention it I'd say: "All right, if you want to tell me a dream you can." And then he would go on to something else.

He tried to lie on the couch once because the other actor lies down. He figured this out because the table is closer to the couch than to the chair. But he couldn't remain lying down. He simply couldn't say a word that way. So he sat up. Now, for the past two sessions, he will talk a little, then he will lean forward and he will put his hand over his mouth and not say anything. Last session he came in and said: "I don't like for you to probe me." I asked him what he meant and he said: "Well, when you ask me a question, that means you're probing." I suggested that to him a question is an attack, because if I were to say to him: "Is it nice outside?" he'd say: "What do you mean is it nice outside? What are you trying to find out?"

DR. REIK: I wonder about you. Do you sometimes look in the mirror? Why do you have such a low opinion of yourself? What the hell is that? He put his hand to his mouth because he doesn't want to say three words. It is your function to tell him that. You have to say: "Look here," what's his name, John or so, "You have fallen in love." Well, you don't say it quite this way, you say: "You kick against falling in love with me."

DR. FREEMAN: Well, I asked him once if he would be very distressed if in addition to being angry with me, he found out that he also had some positive feelings.

DR. REIK: No, Erika.

DR. FREEMAN: Last time he told me: "I think you need a lot of help." So I said: "What kind?" And he said: "I don't think you know what's going on, and you don't know what to do with yourself until I come here. And then I know you are all right because I'm here to help you. Furthermore, I think you are in love with me." I guess that proves your point. His projection seems to prove it.

DR. REIK: Yes, he put the shoe on the other foot. But in order to, how should I say, to spare his feelings, you say: "You fight against it."

DR. FREEMAN: Then that is the reason he won't talk, that is the resistance?

DR. REIK: Of course it is. That is a great resistance. You have to constantly be aware that the resistances are very often hidden even to the patient himself or herself. So you have to open up the resistance. I give you an instance from a supervision analysis of mine. The analyst reported about a girl patient she had, much younger than she. I had absolute conviction that the patient had a strong resistance against this analyst, and that the analyst had overlooked it. So, I asked her: "Has the patient resistance?" "No," she said. "Well, did the girl remark on your dress?" Girls always remark on how people dress. "Or how the room looks?" "No, she never said anything." "Well," I said, "there must be some hidden resistance." So I told her she should insist upon it in the next session.

DR. FREEMAN: Insist upon what?

DR. REIK: Upon getting an answer to the question: "What have you got against me?" So she asked, and the patient said: "Nothing." But a few minutes before the end of the session, the patient said: "Yesterday, when I left here, I thought about you. I know that you work seven hours a day. I know that you are not married. But you want to get your Ph.D., and so you have to go to school and your time is filled. And I said to myself: 'Oh, God, I hope I don't become like her.' " The greatest resistance which is possible.

DR. FREEMAN: Because it was dangerous to identify with her analyst in such a case.

DR. REIK: Yes. But she should identify.

DR. FREEMAN: But if she sees her analyst as an unfulfilled person then it must frighten her.

DR. REIK: Yes. "Oh God, I shouldn't become like her." So you have to be prepared for hidden resistances. And this fellow, your patient, is fighting against falling in love with you. Then later on you would go into sexual things.

DR. FREEMAN: Another time when he couldn't say anything at all, I said: "Look at the room. There are a lot of paintings, sculpture, books, all kinds of things. Look at the desk, what do you see?" And he said: "I'm not going to talk about that. That pen is a phallic symbol." So I said: "All right, if you are not ready to talk about it, we won't talk about it."

DR. REIK: On the contrary, I would say: "You have to talk about it. It occurred to you, so you must say it. That is our gentleman's agreement," I would say jokingly, "to tell everything."

DR. FREEMAN: I said something like that. But I also said: "Look, you chose to mention the pen, you could have chosen the book." So he yelled: "I knew you were going to force me to do this and I'm not going to. You are forcing me and I won't."

DR. REIK: So, he is repeating a sadistic-masochistic trend; as with the fights with his girl friend.

DR. FREEMAN: Yes, and he often tries to embroil me in this kind of interaction.

Dr. Reik: You have to be aware of that. You have to repeat that. It is only verbally a sadistic-masochistic fight.

Dr. Freeman: I'll tell you the dream he brought yesterday, in the sequence he did. He said: "First I'll give you my interpretation. I have an uncle who is an alcoholic."

Dr. Reik: Is that the dream or is that interpretation?

Dr. Freeman: That is his interpretation. He insisted upon giving me his *a priori* interpretation before he would even part with the dream.

Dr. Reik: Ah, yes. So tell me. He said: "I have an uncle who is an alcoholic."

Dr. Freeman: Yes. "And when I was little he used to give me a dollar when he was drunk. And I liked the idea of getting a dollar, but I always felt that he didn't really know what he was doing, because he is drunk, so maybe I shouldn't take it. Also he was married to a woman who looked like you. I don't know if he is still married to her." And then he said: "But this is my dream. My aunt and uncle were in the process of moving and among their things I noticed a box. I took the box and I opened it and in it were many shiny diamonds and lots of money in coins. And I took one dollar's worth of coins." He could think of nothing else to say after he told me this, except to repeat that his uncle was an alcoholic.

Then he said: "I don't know what my problem is with money, but it makes me very uncomfortable when I talk to *you* about money." So I said: "But we have to discuss that too." And he said: "I don't want there to be money between us. Between you and me." I said: "But between you and me there is money. After all, you pay me the fee which we set." He said: "But I don't want you to get angry with me." So I answered: "I have no reason to be angry with you." Then he said: "Well, how come you don't react to what I say?" So I asked: "What kind of reaction do you want me to have?" "I don't know," he said. "How do I know you won't get angry every time I express my feeling?" So I asked him why he thought I should be angry with him.

DR. REIK: No, Erika. I tell you, unconsciously he does not want to discuss money with you. His giving you money means to him that he puts you on the same level as a whore. You know, I was in Mohawk last summer for my vacation. I stayed in a Quaker hotel and the waitresses there were students from Vassar. One of them who studied French literature liked to talk with me in French. Once she said: "*Je suis une fille.*" She meant "girl," and that is what the word literally means in French. But in Paris it means a prostitute. And so it is here, Erika. This man cannot talk money with you, because it equates you to a whore.

DR. FREEMAN: Well, I wouldn't force him to talk about it. But he brought up the topic of money and then at the end of the session he brought it up again to be sure, because he doesn't think he owes me much money at all.

DR. REIK: He has a resistance against giving you money. Which means on the one side he doesn't want to miss the money, but on the other side is the unconscious. Significant. So he was stealing in the dream. And in general stealing has the unconscious significance of a substitute for something sexual. The boys who steal from their mother's purse, a few pennies? Forbidden sexual activity with mother.

DR. FREEMAN: Why only one dollar? What is the significance of that?

DR. REIK: His uncle used to give him one dollar.

DR. FREEMAN: Does that mean that he has an unconscious attraction for his uncle's wife?

DR. REIK: Yes, I would say so. He compares her to you. Do you have a counter-transference? Do you find him very attractive?

DR. FREEMAN: I don't find him attractive as a male. He's like a young round boy.

DR. REIK: Is he·fat?

DR. FREEMAN: Not really, but he gives that impression. Incidentally, he said: "I decided to get fat, because fat actors are always working." "Who says that?" I asked. "Well, you don't know them," he said. "They are supporting actors, but they are always working."

DR. REIK: Yes. Ask him once whether he knew that the first and most prominent actor of Hamlet was fat. I don't remember his name, it was in beginning of the seventeen hundreds. It is so paradoxical—none of us could imagine Hamlet as fat. What parts does he get?

DR. FREEMAN: Until now he's been getting juvenile leads. He's not the leading man type. I guess that also tells you about my counter-transference.

DR. REIK: Yes. Well, I would interpret the dream as something sexual. Forbidden things towards his aunt or respectively you.

Look, Erika, you know that in dream interpretation you have to use the associations of the patients all the time, and you have to tell them about the symbolism in dreams. But the other thing the patient doesn't know is, of course, the resistance, or the transference in general, positive to negative.

DR. FREEMAN: Do you always interpret dreams?

DR. REIK: No, sometimes a dream cannot be interpreted. You can come back to it at a later time in the analysis. Weeks later. You compare a dream to a tablecloth. You cannot always take off the cloth entirely. It is sometimes enough that you lift the corner to see what is under it, because a dream interpretation can go on for many hours.

Consider also that some of this patient's dreams have to do with you. You have to redirect the analysis around your person. In general you could say the following: A person comes to analysis because he has a certain neurosis. And during analysis this neurosis changes its character into a transference neurosis in which everything centers around the person of the analyst.

DR. FREEMAN: Incidentally, he is very similar to another patient who used to be a teacher.

DR. REIK: What did he teach?

DR. FREEMAN: Elementary school. He liked it very much, but he stopped teaching because whenever summer vacation started and all the children were away, he missed them so much he could hardly stand it. He didn't want to start the same thing all over again every year.

DR. REIK: I treated three teachers in America. And they had something in common. They were unconsciously, unconsciously I say, latently, partly homosexual, and they were sadistic. And when I talked about that in one of these analyses the patient was not as astonished as I thought he would be. He said: "Oh, I knew that somewhere in my mind." The other day I saw a book in a window with the title: *The Child, Our Enemy*, by a teacher. But of course, in order to want to educate, you have to be slightly aggressive and sadistic—only *psychically*, of course.

DR. FREEMAN: But now when this patient wakes up in the morning he is very upset because he could have been teaching and making money.

DR. REIK: He has no money?

DR. FREEMAN: No.

DR. REIK: And he doesn't do anything at home? Reading and so?

DR. FREEMAN: No. He has been trying to write, but he's having trouble with it. Partly because his whole family thinks he is crazy for wanting to write.

DR. REIK: What are the brothers?

DR. FREEMAN: One doctor and one architect.
He said he suffered a nervous breakdown when he was
a very young man. I asked him what he meant by a
nervous breakdown. And he told me that while he was on
vacation his parents sold their house—the one he had
grown up in—and they bought another one. He never got
used to the new one, so he would keep going back to
the old neighborhood. And he became very depressed.

DR. REIK: That is interesting on account of the following. It is very well known that women get a depression
when they change their apartment. I remember my first
wife, she was my childhood love, and we were married
young. Later on I got into practice and got a better apartment and my wife cried when she left the old apartment.
Even though the new one was better, she cried. But it is
clear why, because a woman is so connected with her
apartment, with her home. That is specifically a feminine
trait. Nothing to be compared with men. The depression
over changing of an apartment or a house is always
feminine.

DR. FREEMAN: For a while he worked at a job that
allowed him to get to know the people in the new neighborhood. This was how he earned the money and came
out of his depression.

DR. REIK: I would say this was significant, because of
the social thing, and that is feminine. I give you an instance. When my daughter was in college, it was at
Bennington, she had to earn money. She had to prove that
she can earn money. And I wanted to get her a job with
my publisher. But she absolutely did not want that. She
said she cannot stand being alone in a cubicle, she has to
be with people. So she got a job at Gimbels. And the
ladies who buy there chased her around. And she always
came home as if she would drop dead, so tired was she.

Nevertheless, she said she wants to be with people, she cannot stand to be alone. That is a feminine trait. Most women have it.

DR. FREEMAN: It sometimes seems to me as though as analysts we have some kind of modified schizoid reaction. You cannot bring your own problems or concerns to the sessions, unless that too can be used as food for the patient's development. So I find that as soon as a patient walks into my office, I can cut all my personal moods away.

DR. REIK: Yes, one must not let one's own mood touch the patient. But I give you an instance of what happened with another analyst. His wife was near delivery of their child and so he didn't sleep. Three nights he sat with her at home and didn't sleep. Finally at five one morning she said: "Now I better go to the hospital." So he took her in the car and stayed with her at the hospital from five in the morning to one o'clock in the afternoon. A long process. At three o'clock he had a patient. The patient turned around and said to him: "You are asleep. You're not interested in me. You don't give a damn about me. You fall asleep when I talk." And this analyst denied it, instead of saying what he should say, namely: "Look here, I didn't sleep last night because my wife just had a baby." I told him, "It was an extraordinary situation. After all, you are not supposed to be a superman. You are a human being too." Freud said in such cases you have to tell the truth to the patient.

I remember when I lived in the Hague, I treated a lady psychiatrist. It was a training analysis. She was very attractive by the way, only not my type, so to speak. Between you and me, she was a snob. For instance she talked in the analytic hour about the *orificium uteri*. She used technical terms all the time. She was a physician, of course. And she got into a fight, into a strong resistance with me. I'll tell you about the nature of the resistance later on. It happened that one morning at nine o'clock, when she had an hour scheduled with me, I took a walk. I had entirely forgotten about her. I went walking on the Scheveningen Broadwalk, that is near the Hague. So when I came back to my office she was waiting there. Freud told me later on: "In this case, you have to say, 'I didn't like to see you.' You have to be careful how you do it, but you have to tell the patient the truth." This is the counter-transference.

But I'll tell you something else that happened with this lady psychiatrist. I had been living in the Hague for three years by then and in an unguarded moment during her analytic hour, I said: "The citizens of the Hague are so '*burgerlijk*.' " *Burgerlijk* in Dutch means sort of pedestrian, or Philistine, you know? I said that during the analytic hour and she couldn't forget it, nor forgive it. She was a great Dutch patriot and she got into a terrible resistance. It was towards summer when I went on vacation and she went on vacation. Finally she said: "We can't settle this. Let's go to Vienna, to Freud." So I went with her to Vienna. Same train, different cars, of course. We didn't talk. And when we arrived there, we sat in the waiting room of Freud, together, without speaking.

He opened the door from his office and called me in first, because I had prepared him that there is a conflict between a patient and me and that we wanted his judgment in the matter. He said to me: "Did anything dramatic happen?" I looked at him without any understanding. And then it dawned on me, it was something I would never have dreamed of. He meant had I gotten into an affair with her. But she was absolutely not my type. She was very unfriendly, and after all, in analysis with me. So I said: "God, no." Then I told him the story. He called her in and in her presence he said: "Reik was absolutely wrong. When you are living in a country and you use the hospitality of that country you cannot dare to make such offending remarks about the people. Reik will apologize."

DR. FREEMAN: And he instructed you in front of the patient to apologize?

DR. REIK: Yes, and I did.

DR. FREEMAN: How did you feel?

DR. REIK: Terrible. But he was right. When you live in a country and you are received with great honors there and you accept the hospitality—I had come from Austria, of course—you cannot offend the citizens of the country. And if you do, you have to admit that you did something wrong. Afterwards the analysis went very well, very well. The next summer we even took vacation together in Altausee in the Saltzkammergut and she made the acquaintance of Beer-Hoffman.

DR. FREEMAN: You mean you went on vacation at the same time.

DR. REIK: Yes, as friends. Several years ago I met her in Amsterdam where I was sitting in the Congress of the Dutch analysts. In the meantime she had three children. And she was very nice, very friendly.

Tell me about some of your other patients.

DR. FREEMAN: Well, one of my patients is divorced, and she asked me whether I thought she was in love with her boyfriend. So I asked her to describe how she felt and she said, that for one thing, she finds it very difficult to stay away from him. She feels lost when he isn't there. I asked her if he felt the same way, and she said she didn't know. He doesn't say anything, but since he is a very shy person he doesn't like to spend very much time with anyone. So, he just calls her and he sometimes comes to visit and they sit and talk, just talk. I asked her what her fantasies were and she said she doesn't have any fantasies.

DR. REIK: No sexual fantasies?

DR. FREEMAN: No.

DR. REIK: No, why should she? She should have fantasies of tenderness and affection.

DR. FREEMAN: She has fantasies of having his child.

DR. REIK: What was her sex life before?

DR. FREEMAN: Average American.

DR. REIK: What is that? Does she reach an orgasm? I ask that in the first interview. I have an interview today, with a lady I never saw, but I am sure I shall ask her that. Does she reach an orgasm in sexual intercourse? Does she masturbate and whether she reaches an orgasm in masturbation? Does she have any extra-marital relations, and so on. How long have you had this patient?

DR. FREEMAN: About two weeks. She seems very eager to talk about anything very intellectual, but when it comes to sex, it's hands off.

DR. REIK: How old is she?

DR. FREEMAN: Thirty-one.

DR. REIK: What was the reason for the divorce?

DR. FREEMAN: Adultery. He fell in love with someone else. She said that she doesn't really mind, because when she married him, it was more for security than for love. And because her mother approved of him, since he came from a wealthy family and had a good name— the usual reasons why mothers approve. I think that probably part of the syndrome is based on the fact that she always did what her mother wanted her to do, because she had to be a nice girl, respectful and respectable. This is probably one of her problems right now, that nice girls don't have affairs. Now, I can't really say anything, because I don't know enough yet. But she insists that my attitude is the same as hers.

DR. REIK: It is possible. One woman understands the

other. We could say that one woman understands all women in the world, except one—herself. Sometimes she is absolutely without understanding of herself.

DR. FREEMAN: When I ask her anything about her sex life she begins to answer, but then she always goes on to something else. The first time she brought up sex by herself was when she started to talk about this young man. He's younger than she is, about twenty-four or twenty-five.

DR. FREEMAN: Well, certain types search for older women.

DR. REIK: Is that pathology on his part?

DR. FREEMAN: It is not necessarily pathological. Think that Disraeli, Lord Beaconsfield, married a woman much older, which I mentioned. It was a good marriage.

DR. FREEMAN: This patient is afraid because her first husband too was younger than she was. Her mother said that it would be all right. But because of this patient's own middle class attitude, the man must be older. Now this man is much younger than she is, and she is worried about what it means.

DR. REIK: Perhaps she has motherly feelings towards him. Of taking care of him.

DR. FREEMAN: That might explain why there are no sexual fantasies.

DR. REIK: Perhaps she hides her sexual fantasies from herself and from you.

DR. FREEMAN: Behind her maternal wishes. Is this a fairly common defense among women?

DR. REIK: That is an exception. My sister, who is two years younger than I, has a habit. She empties and cleans all ashtrays. So I sit here and smoke, and so she cleans the ashtray the next moment. Sometimes I say: "Why do you go out? Why don't you stay here the whole day and do nothing but that?" What she carries on is maternal.

For instance with the laundry, I have to have every day everything new—shirts and socks and so on. So I have said: "That is nonsense. You want to make me as you are. So I insist I have to have a new shirt and new pants and new socks morning and noon and evening. Three times a day." So I make fun of her but not in a bad way.

DR. FREEMAN: What does it indicate about a man if he violently objects.

DR. REIK: He is resisting his unconscious incestuous wishes. So his wife would be clever to disguise her maternal feelings and not to show them.

DR. REIK: Tell me some more about your other patients.

DR. FREEMAN: There is a patient who has developed a habit. This is a man, another actor, in his late twenties, living with a girl of his own age. He is very promiscuous. His father doesn't approve of this girl at all, but he knows that she lives with him. Up until now, every time the patient saw his father he fought with him. He talked to him like a big man, like a successful actor. But what has begun to happen lately when he sees his father, is that he "yesses" him. He says: "I'll do what you say, I won't marry her, I'll invest money." He says he doesn't act like a big successful person anymore. And he has been making approaches to his father. He calls him and asks: "What are you doing tomorrow?" If the father says: "I'm playing golf," my patient asks: "Can I come along?" He's never done this sort of thing before.

But recently every time he sees his father, he gets depressed. He comes away with a feeling of sadness which he never had before. He came to the last session all dressed up. He used to lie on the couch and for the past two weeks he's been sitting up. This time he sat up and said that on his way to the sessions he got very nauseous, but didn't know what it was. But it went away and he was afraid that the reason he got nauseated was that he had slept with a girl the night before.

Dr. Reik: With another girl?

Dr. Freeman: Yes, with another girl. And the reason he got nauseous was that he would have to confess it to me. He didn't want to tell me about it, but he felt he had to. At this session he was dressed up to see still another girl who had just come into town. She was the daughter of a very influential man and he'd had an affair with her at another time, in another place. After the session he was going to sleep with her. He felt very badly because he felt he was being unfaithful to his present girl friend, and he was afraid of what would happen if she found out. I asked him: "Why are you going to sleep with this other girl?" And he said: "I'm going to sleep with her because she is a famous woman. She is a beautiful woman. She is very successful, her father is very successful, and I want to show her that even so, anybody can have her." Then there was a long silence and he said: "I didn't know it was going to be so easy. How come you didn't stop me?" I said: "I'm concerned with what you do and why you do things and not with moralizing." But I had the distinct feeling that he was very upset with me for not saying to him: "Don't do that."

Dr. Reik: Yes, that was the right technique. It could be a case of the father.

Dr. Freeman: Then he said he wants to have four sessions a week. He's been bringing it up now for a number of weeks and I told him I would let him know whether I had time or not.

Dr. Reik: Now he comes only twice a week?

Dr. Freeman: Yes. Originally he said he was only to come once. His first request for coming four times a week had at its root not therapy but a seductive move. He has, among other things, the sense that he is in control of everything. The analyst who referred him to me treated his girl friend. The patient said that the reason he didn't want to see his girl friend's analyst was that he felt he could take over anytime during the sessions. The reason he came to me was because there was going to be no "monkey business." It would mean analysis and work and that's all. However, as of now he still wants to come four times a week. When I told him I'd have to check my schedule, he said: "But I'm your only patient. How come if I have time, you don't have time? You don't have anything else to do besides seeing me."

DR. REIK: It is interesting that so many of your male patients have to think they are the only one.

DR. FREEMAN: Yes. And then he remarked that everyone he knows is in love with him. He thinks that maybe I am too and he expects that any minute now I will begin to conform to the behavior of his girl friend's analyst, who is a very loving person. Then he said: "Besides, what's the point of paying a lot of money for an analyst, if I can't at least sometimes get to sleep with her." So I suggested that since he is coming to me for analysis, that's fine. But if there are other services he wants, there are people who handle that for pay.

DR. REIK: Yes.

DR. FREEMAN: He was furious and stalked out of my office. I have the feeling that he might not come back, but I'm not sure.

DR. REIK: I think he will. But I tell you something. The man must have strong unconscious homosexual tendencies.

DR. FREEMAN: Yes. In part because he sleeps with so many people. . . .

DR. REIK: Not only that, but because of his depression

after he goes away from father. That means: "I would like to impress you because of my achievements, but I cannot." So the real thing is the father.

Dr. Freeman: I said that to him a while back. He used to go to another analyst, a man who interpreted that money means masculinity to him. He used to be very fat, and his father would always say: "I don't know if you're going to grow up to be a man or a woman," because he had rather heavy breast development when he was little, but then he lost it.

Dr. Reik: Is he attractive?

Dr. Freeman: Yes.

Dr. Reik: What is the father?

Dr. Freeman: He married for money. His mother came from a rich family. She died when he was eleven. When he was little and fat, his mother would stand him in front of a mirror to show him how much nicer he would look if he lost weight. He said he always felt somehow that this was some kind of sexual contact. He also had a crush on his mother's friend and he thought that loving her was like having a relationship with his mother. He was less than ten at the time.

In the beginning of his treatment he wasn't overtly hostile to women. He always spoke of how much he loved them, and what an experienced lover he was, and how wonderful they thought he was. I thought that basically he was hostile towards women. I have the feeling that his suggestion about sleeping with the analyst which was supposedly made in jest, was a hostile attack.

Dr. Reik: Yes, everything which takes away from analysis is attack.

Dr. Freeman: And I thought this specific direction was even more of an attack because of his unconscious hostility towards women.

Dr. Reik: Yes, that's right. I would say that. And I

would say to him that he is unconsciously hostile, since that is functional. If someone is hostile to the one sex, he is unconsciously attracted to the other sex. They call that Reik's law, because I formulated it. That means if I am very hostile to women, then I am unconsciously attracted to men. If I am hostile to men, I am attracted to women. It is a functional relationship. Mention it to him in relationship to the transference—but only in relationship to you.

DR. FREEMAN: In other words if he is hostile to me. . . .

DR. REIK: Yes, unconsciously he wants to impress his father, or other actors, or directors, and so on.

DR. FREEMAN: Now another problem is that his first analyst was very friendly, very giving.

DR. REIK: By the rule you are to act different from the previous analyst. Don't do that which the first analyst did, but analyze the relationship between him and the first analyst. The second analyst should behave in the opposite way of the first analyst.

❦

DR. FREEMAN: This is the dream of a man in his thirties, three children. And three marriages. His parents were divorced when he was small. He perceived his mother as a poor helpless thing that had to be taken care of. He had a well-paying job, but a week after I left for my holiday, he stopped working.

DR. REIK: That is perhaps due to your leaving, a kind of punishment.

DR. FREEMAN: Yes. After I returned he began to work again. This is a dream he had shortly before he started work again: "Jesus was being buried in a kind of sloppy way. He was a little exposed even after He was buried. And when I complained that they hadn't buried Him

properly, someone said that some of the dirt had rolled
off when they covered Him. His whole body was black
and the exposed area, which was part of the shoulder
and part of his face, was showing." The only association
he had to this was that he thinks he had another dream
in which he went into a hotel room and there on the
floor was a kind of cocoon, which he watched. And as
he watched it, it opened up and it became bugs. That
frightened him. He had no other associations at all.

DR. REIK: Well, the bugs could be a delivery of a
child.

DR. FREEMAN: Yes, it could well be. His wife is pregnant.

DR. REIK: But there is no material for the Jesus image?

DR. FREEMAN: No.

DR. REIK: In general I would say that it might be a
displacement of the genitals from below to above, to the
shoulder and the face. But we can't say anything more,
because we don't know enough about him.

DR. FREEMAN: He did say that he had a brief affair
with a black girl and he was afraid to talk about it, because he was afraid that I would disapprove. I was wonder-
ing though, in so many cases they are afraid of punishment from me. Not that their wives will find out.

DR. REIK: Have a sort of sovereign attitude towards
that.

DR. FREEMAN: Yes, I do. But what are the dynamics?

DR. REIK: Father, father. It goes back to the Oedipus
situation. He is afraid of father and displaces it onto you.
Freud always told us that, let us say, a mother threatens
a little boy because he plays with himself sexually.
Nevertheless, although mother is there to intimidate him,
it is father of whom he is afraid. Father fulfills there a
phylogenetic function.

DR. FREEMAN: In other words even though the actual

threat comes from the female, the little boy experiences it as coming from the male.

DR. REIK: Yes.

DR. FREEMAN: So, in effect, I represent the father to them.

DR. REIK: Right, right. And that is what the transference consists of, in part.

DR. FREEMAN: Another of my patients had a fight with his fiancee and he said he wanted to stop analysis because he didn't want to have to handle any more of her problems.

DR. REIK: Why did you not encourage him? In general if there is an argument it is almost a fifty-fifty proposition. The girl must be feeling guilty too.

DR. FREEMAN: I asked him why he thought it was his doing if they had a fight. Her problem may have played into his and vice versa, and that might be the reason for the friction. He said that he didn't really know, but that he didn't want to be in analysis any more because it makes him too much aware of her problems. Besides she expects him now to be more understanding and to discuss her analysis with him. So I told him that he is not

to discuss analysis. If there is anything she wants to talk about she is to talk to her own analyst, but he is not available to be her analyst. This seemed to relieve him.

DR. REIK: That's right, you must encourage him. That it must also be the fault of his girl friend, Jane or whatever her name is—it cannot be only his fault.

DR. REIK: I know you wanted to discuss obsessional neurosis, but I didn't know from what point of view I should do it. Then an accident happened to me. An acquaintance showed me the correspondence between Freud and Pfister, and he said: "Did you see that your name is mentioned there?" I said: "No." I hadn't read the book yet. So he showed that Freud wrote to Pfister: "Don't worry about your American patient. I have here Dr. Reik who is specializing in obsessional neurosis and he had great success with a Russian patient." That was written in 1924. Of course, I enjoyed that. I was in elation that Freud, more than forty years ago, recognized that I specialized in cases of obsessional neurosis and that I had much success with them.

Following that I got in a depression, for many reasons. First I remembered the case of mine that Freud mentioned, a Russian count. Freud had no time to treat him, so he sent him to me with the diagnosis of obsessional neurosis. But after a few months of analysis, the man's parents took him away, and he became schizophrenic. That is not so unusual as you might think, because very often after the superstructure of analysis is taken away there develops a psychosis. You will find in Fenichel, for instance, the following diagnosis: "Case of schizophrenia by way of intensive psychoanalysis kept on the level of obsessional neurosis." That is possible, too. Now, the second reason for my depression was, of course, that I did not live up to the hope which Freud expressed with regard to me, which you could read also in Jones' biography. And the third reason was also something which you will find childish. Since I got old I lost my taste in reading fiction. The only thing I read before falling asleep is Simenon, French detective stories, and I'm still interested in what Monsieur Maigret, that is his leading figure, does there. In connection with that, this Russian count's analysis was preferably led in French, although he knew English, and of course Russian was his mother tongue. And I read in one of the novels of Simenon how Maigret walks on the Boulevard in Paris and he looks at *le Nylons*. I couldn't understand what that was, but I found out later that *"le Nylons"* is a new French expression for women. Now I want to talk about this patient first. He was a young man of twenty-two, a count, Greek-Orthodox, who came to Vienna with his parents to see Freud. Freud had no time to take him and sent him to me. I should have been suspicious from my first visit with this man, because he received me with the following words: "Satan and Beelzebub were just there and asked me if I want *frikassee de veau, Kalbfleish.*" Now that was strange enough that Satan should ask him such a thing. Later on it became clear that he meant the butler and the servant had been there and had asked him that. When you hear it, it is prophetic enough. Nevertheless, it made good sense. Namely, his parents were snobs who considered only aristocrats their equals and treated all servants brutally. He remembered his father once hit a servant or a butler. So he figured it this way; since it is necessary that you treat the devil or Satan badly, these people whom his father mistreated must be devils. So, for instance, he said the "girl devil," and he meant the chambermaid, because she belonged to the servant class. While he sometimes spoke of the Holy Virgin as the elegant Lady—the opposite, of course.

Now why did his parents want him to go into analysis? Because he also suffered under blasphemous thoughts. He was compelled to think blasphemous thoughts about those persons who were most sacred to him. When, for instance, he thought of The Last Supper he thought "drunkards," or often about the Holy Virgin, "whore," or that Christ was the son of a carpenter and therefore He was nothing. Whenever he thought something of this kind he hit himself with his fist against his head, so that his forehead was always bloody. The first thing that Freud told me was that I should prevent him from harming himself.

The interesting thing is that he thought Christ was very clever, (he called him *reynard*), while people who are lower are stupid. To his astonishment when he now thought of the symbol of Christ, there appeared to him the face of his father, whom he considered stupid. He also brought God in connection with evacuation, and asked himself if the great Christ also had a movement of the bowels. Now for as long as he could not answer that, he put a penance on himself that he should have no movement of the bowels for as long as possible. But when he had to make a movement of the bowels he wondered whether the toilet paper is not the Gospel, the New Testament. Now you could imagine, he was there in the toilet with two very uncomfortable choices: if he wipes himself he commits a terrible blasphemy because the paper is the Gospel, or should he remain unwiped, that is to say, dirty.

Also he came to the following consideration, which is typically obsessional. What is the difference between a gentleman and a waiter. The difference is that a gentleman wears a white tie with his formal dress while a waiter wears a black tie. That is a characteristic displacement to a detail. To give you an instance of how that worked, he said: "There are three aristocrats in heaven and two lackeys in hell. Namely, in Heaven are God, Jesus Christ, and the Holy Ghost, while in hell are Satan and Beelzebub." But very often he reversed the thought. He was taught to think that the whore is the wife of the devil, but the Virgin is the Mother of God. But through compulsion to reverse that, he would think that the whore became the wife of God and the Virgin the mother of the devil.

It was interesting that though at the time he spoke French, he sometimes spoke English. It was, so to speak, a geographical device, depending upon when the thought first came, from which soil it came, because he learned English much later. You remember Jones once treated an obsessional patient who was compelled to think every thought to its end; to the extreme final end. And then he had to think of the opposite and then he had to find a medium between these two.

Slowly there developed a language between this Russian count and me which was not understandable for others. For instance, we spoke about the sacred Prince Oldenburg service, which meant the Mass. He said: "I am the Duke of Hohenberg, who takes vengeance on the sins of the fathers." You see he gave the name of aristocrats, instead of the name of God. So that if someone would come in (I had to come to his hotel, because he could not go out into the street), they would, of course, think that we are two crazy people speaking together. Maybe you remember I once told on that television show of David Susskind—it was not a formal program, we sat around and drank coffee, talked unprepared, and we kidded each other. I made there a remark that if in the tenth century or so someone said he met the devil on the street, it was accepted. But if today you say you met the devil on the corner of Seventy-ninth Street and Broadway, you would go to an insane asylum. So it's a cultural difference, a time difference, if you want. The Holy Ghost, for instance, in order to differentiate, this patient spoke of *oiseaux vulgaires*, and *oiseaux de réseau*, vulgar birds and aristocratic birds.

Dr. FREEMAN: Did you get him to stop hitting himself, to stop hurting himself?

Dr. REIK: Yes. The reason he obeyed was positive transference, he liked me from the beginning.

Dr. FREEMAN: How did you get him to stop, what did you do?

Dr. REIK: I said to him: "Don't do that."

DR. FREEMAN: Did he ever hit himself again?

DR. REIK: Yes, But when he did do that later on, it was in defiance of me. I mentioned that he couldn't leave his room, because those thoughts were always present. When he went into the street and he saw a restaurant, he thought it was a miracle of Jesus Christ, and immediately the thought came as a blasphemy.

But these blasphemous thoughts became so overpowering that his parents decided they should take him away from Vienna. And the end was that he got into such grotesque thoughts which are not really obsessional, they already belong to the realm of schizophrenic syndrome. I give you an instance. There was in his room an old armchair, and he associated it with his father because his father also sat in that chair. Then he had the thought that a golden chair writes in his album. He had a graphological album which famous people autographed. But the thought of an elegant armchair writing in an album sounds crazy.

And connected with this, with the association there is sometimes between religion and obsessional thoughts, I knew in Vienna a very religious Jew, who wanted that the gaslight should be turned off at a certain time on the Sabbath eve. Now in general, the Orthodox Jews brought in a Gentile to turn it off. But this man thought you should not tempt any person to do such a thing. So he did the following. He put this gaslight in connection with a clock, and if the clock said nine o'clock then it turned the light off. He was sort of outwitting God, because he didn't do it, the machinery did it. An arising of blasphemous thought occurs in the middle of warding off a temptation.

Anatole France once told the following story. He spoke about the easy manner in which Italian priests converse in church. After a Mass, a mother with her child went up to speak with the priest and the child thought there is a flower there and wanted to touch the Holy Ghost. And you know you cannot touch a Holy Ghost, so the priest took away the child's hand, but the baby persisted in touching. Finally the priest said to the child: *"Kaka"* which is, of course, a bad word.

Also in connection with religion and obsessional thought, I wanted to show you an analogy here between a modern, clear-thinking woman and ancient religious thoughts. This lady, who didn't think in any way religiously, loved to play patience. You know that card game? So she said, "If the heart knave comes from this place then everything'll be all right with my lover. If on the other hand the knave of diamonds goes there, my husband will find out about my affair." She was using the cards, so to speak, as a modern oracle. She avoided the most important question by not raising it. And that's exactly what the old Greeks and Babylonians did 2500 years before her time. For instance, when Cyrus the King wanted to find out whether he should go to war with Persia he went to the oracle of Delphi and the priestess answered, "If Cyrus does that he will destroy a great country." And that he did—his own. And there you have the ambiguousness of the oracle. And that ambiguousness was in this woman's case too. For instance, she said to herself: "Will my analysis be finished in a year?" A year by which calendar? There was the Jewish calendar, the Catholic calendar. So she never came to a decision about that. Or her doubt began in the wording. For instance: "Will my treatment be finished?" Then came the doubt: "Do I treat Reik or does Reik treat me?"

You see, the doubt serves the following purpose. People with obsessional thoughts want to find certainty in life, and there is absolutely no certainty. And they know that, so they are ambivalent. Therefore they ask questions in whose nature it is that there cannot be a certainty. Let's

say, time. They destroy every watch they have, because
that would be a certainty. But the clocks differ, of course,
in different places. Or they think on the question of who
is the father or the mother of somebody. That is the great
comparison with religious dogma, because there were for
centuries arguments if Jesus is of the same substance as
God, or similar substance, or unlike substance, or a substance which is entirely different. The real deepest fight is,
of course, whether I love or hate. The deepest doubt. And
hate comes always into it.

You know, I did not at first consider the count psychotic, though I had a surprising reaction. I had a visiting
card from Freud which had written on it," *Zwangsneu-
rose.* Full treatment." I did that, of course. Today, I certainly would not simply take the word of a reputable
colleague of a diagnosis after one interview. But this was
Freud, and I was very young, and I was awed by him.
But without the diagnosis from Freud at that time I
would have first considered this patient was psychotic.

But that is not astonishing. Think of the difference
between a psychosis and a neurosis. A man has compul-
sions. He cannot sit down on the chair. Why not? Because he is afraid of spirochete. He washes the chair with
alcohol, that is a measure of protection. But is his view
really that he could be infected by the spirochete? The
answer is yes and no. He has two opinions. On one side
he thinks: "I'm really afraid of that," and on the other
side he knows that is all nonsense. But if this man says:
"I cannot sit down on this chair because my behind is
made of glass, and I shatter that if I sit," then he has given
up reality.

For instance, there is no doubt about the obsessional
character of Jones's case, the one who followed an idea
to its logical end, then to the opposite, and then to the
middle of it. That is not a schizophrenic. If you think of

the number obsession, someone counts how many books are there, to see if it is an odd or even number. There is the story about Anton Bruckner, the composer, perhaps the greatest modern besides Mahler, and he suffered under an obsessional neurosis. He went once with a train to Kloster-Neuburg, that is perhaps half an hour by train from Vienna, and while the train stopped for a moment he counted the windows of a house there. But because he wasn't sure he counted right, he had to get out of the train and walk one hour to go back to count them again. Or when he was a professor already in the Vienna Conservatory, he was at a banquet and across from him was a young lady with pearls. Suddenly without any preparation he stuck out a finger and he touched one of the pearls on her necklace, because he was not sure whether he had counted the pearls correctly. And he had to make sure—to the indignation of all present. You know Bruckner was also a very religious Catholic. But he had a very strange thing—he was ashamed of being Catholic, namely when he was confronting someone who came from Vienna. Once a professor of music history visited him in St. Florian where he was at home. They took a walk and it was a terribly cold winter month. So while they were walking the bells of the church rang out, and of course Bruckner had to take off his hat, and he said: "It is so terribly hot today." Which was nonsense, it was terribly cold.

The obsessional thoughts were in the case of the Russian count a defense against his father. He thought of God as a fox and his father as an ass. And this gray hair of his father came to him as though it were on a donkey or something you know? So in order to avoid thoughts about his father, he thought about God. But sometimes he confused the two. He avoided thoughts about his mother too.

I think of another case. Freud sent to me someone who was very strange. It was an American, and I thought he was a case of obsessional neurosis. But after three months of analysis, in Vienna that meant five days a week, the man all of a sudden said that men come over the roof into his room and want to castrate him. That, then, was paranoia—that was quite clear.

Sometimes an obsessional thought occurs to you and you don't understand why. A patient of mine in Vienna had the idea, why should he not drink out of the chamberpot of his grandmother.

Dr. Freeman: If he thought it, it was obsessive—if he did it, it was compulsive.

Dr. Reik: Yes. There is certainly a great connection between obsessive and compulsive. About the chamberpot idea. He heard that a German *Minnesinger*—you know a minstrel, troubador—did that with a lady. In other cases there is no doubt. For instance, in the case of this lady who used patience as an oracle. There is no doubt that that was a compulsion. She lost many hours of every day playing patience, and always avoiding the real question.

Dr. Freeman: How about the treatment of an ordinary obsessive?

Dr. Reik: Well, there is a good chance that you can cure him. When you succeed to bring the patient without too great resistance to accept the repressed as part of his personality. That is what the analyst does. He takes the repressed, the disavowed, the denied into the framework of emotional and mental processes and makes the patient recognize that it is a part of his personality and he has to live with it. What cannot be cured has to be endured. It is part of his personality that he has hostility and hate and so on. As everybody has.

Dr. Freeman: Do you place importance on the content of the obsessional thinking?

Dr. Reik: Oh, yes. I give you an instance. One patient went to a lamppost and he had the thought should he go before the lamppost or behind the lamppost? Before the lamppost meant that he is cleverer than a certain cousin of his. Behind the lamppost means he is not as clever as his cousin. He could not go further. He stood there. Couldn't solve the doubt. That is a displacement of something else. There is no help for that entirely. When you once accept that, then it is reasonable, reasonable on a morbid ground. Let me compare it. A man dances with a woman, it is an open dance, and the husband who is paranoid, says: "You are having an affair with this man." The woman says indignantly: "No. How can you say that?" He answers: "You smiled at him." If she says: "No, I did not smile," he would see red and perhaps kill her, because he had seen with his own eyes that she smiled at him. So what can an analyst do? The only thing which an analyst can do is to convince the man that this smiling does not mean that she has an affair. I had here a patient who in the beginning thought which cafeteria should he go to, it was a question of life and death. You have to find out what that means to him and then you have to convince him that it does not in reality mean that. Which is not as simple as it sounds, of course. With the cafeteria problem it was an anal thing—one place charges two cents more than the other, something like that. And from there came, of course, whether he would starve because he had too little money. That then begins to go further. It doesn't stop there.

DR. FREEMAN: Do you remember any other transference interpretation that you made with the count?

DR. REIK: First I had, of course, to take his part against his parents. Especially against his mother, who wanted to be very proud of the cleverness of her son. You see from the examples I gave you how clever he was, how fine his intelligence worked. Second, I spoke his language, namely French. And he felt at ease with me, because he couldn't speak French with the waiters or anyone at the hotel. And then the transference worked slowly into a negative one, because I tried of course to undermine his obsessional system. Then his parents took him away. Freud said you have to develop a gift in yourself, a certain sensitiveness, that you never interpret what the patients say, except when you have the feeling that a few steps and the patient arrives there himself. That is a question of tact. With two exceptions; the first is symptoms in dreams, which is an old acquisition of mankind beyond the knowledge of the singular individual; and the second thing is the beginning of the negative transference.

DR. FREEMAN: One patient I have is always wanting to do something. One day he came to me and said: "My boss has a terrible analyst." So I asked "Why?" He said because that analyst says: "Do this tomorrow. I think you should go into this venture, I think it is a good idea." So he told his boss: "My analyst, wouldn't say that. All she'd say to me is: 'If you think you can do three things at the same time, go ahead.' And then I know I can't do it, because I can't do three things at the same time." But this patient, with the intention of provoking, challenges me, and says: "Tell me what to do."

DR. REIK: The only thing you should say to him is what he should not do if he does something which is self-harming.

When my son was a little boy, he was always having a drum, which he beat. So I said: "Stop that." So he hit it only once more. As if he was stopping that of his own will. Just that once more.

DR. FREEMAN: There is another patient I have who is a very untypical kind of patient. I am tempted to say to her: "Don't." But she is a non-verbal Irish Catholic, with all the stereotype cultural syndromes. Her father was a drunkard and sadistic. He was seventy-eight years old at the time she came to me, and until the previous year he had worked full time doing physical labor. A powerful man, and he would beat her mother. He never permitted lights on in the house, never permitted the radio unless he wanted to hear the news. Everybody was deathly afraid of him, and this patient is deathly afraid of him as well.

Also, she was being used by the family as a servant, she ran all the errands, bought all the presents, very often out of her own money. She lived with two friends in their apartment, but most of her clothes were in her parents' house. So she didn't really live anywhere. And she never carried a pocketbook, only a brown paper bag because she didn't feel that she was worthy of carrying a pocketbook. She has worked at a religious society for ten years at a salary of fifty-nine dollars a week. And being continually exploited. Since she's been with me, her friends got another apartment without her, and she felt guilty about not wanting to move back with her parents whom she hates, at least the father. Desperately afraid of the father because of his drunken rages when he beats everybody. So she didn't want to move back with them, but she was afraid of not being a good daughter. We worked that out. I explained to her that she would be a better daughter if she lived by herself and went to visit them in good spirits, than if she lived there and always felt fear and hatred. So now she lives in an apartment by herself and is happy there.

DR. REIK: How old is she?

DR. FREEMAN: Thirty-seven.

DR. REIK: Virgin?

DR. FREEMAN: Yes. She thought about becoming a nun, but she didn't think she was good enough. Once she went to be tested for aptitude, and said that she would change her job provided she didn't have to learn anything new—no shorthand, nothing. But for the past year and a half she has been attending college at night, and doing very well. She also has a tendency to get little boils, which she always scratches when she gets nervous.

DR. REIK: Something of a masochist.

DR. FREEMAN: Yes. I tried to find out what she thinks about when she scratches. Part of her problem is that everyone is always telling her what to do.

DR. REIK: You should analyze the masochism. Explain to her that she is full of violent feelings.

DR. FREEMAN: I told her this, because I've been trying to get her to accept that fact. But she is extremely religious, and she thinks she shouldn't feel these things. She was referred to me by a Catholic colleague and friend, because, he said: "You're the only analyst I know who won't take her religion away from her."

DR. REIK: Tell her that Christ was using a whip to expel the money lenders from the temple. He was not so meek and mild either.

DR. FREEMAN: I told her: "Look if you're bucking for saint, even the saints were human. What made them saints was not that they didn't have any faults, but what they did for mankind in spite of them." I've been trying to point out to her: "If God puts a feeling into you, a feeling of anger into you, a capacity for anger, then it means that it is meant to be there and is not such terrible feeling, not so despicable."

DR. REIK: What she does is turn it against herself.

DR. FREEMAN: Yes, and I've been trying to get her to turn it against someone else, especially if the other person is being deliberately mean. "But," she says, "you have to be kind to everyone." So I said: "That's right, to every one of God's creatures, and you are one of them.

Therefore, if you mistreat yourself, it is the same sin
as if you mistreat someone else."

Dr. Reik: Yes, very good.

Dr. Freeman: But I never told her to stop scratching.

Dr. Reik: No, no, that would be going too far, because until she has expressed aggressiveness you cannot
do that.

Dr. Freeman: What about sadism? Do you remember
any patients you had who were sadists?

Dr. Reik: Apropos, something occurred to me last time.
One of the first patients Freud sent to me after I returned
from the war was a Baron Dirstein. You can say the name
for two reasons; first, the poor guy was killed by the Nazis
in Vienna, secondly—would you like a mint?

Dr. Freeman: No, thank you.

Dr. Reik:—secondly, he published a book with pictures
by Kokoshka, which is dedicated to me. Now this Dirstein
—his parents got the nobility, his father was *Kriegsliefer-
ant* [one who supplied the army quartermaster]. And this
man, my patient, married during the war, before he became the baron—I think I told this story in *Masochism and
Modern Man*, but it doesn't matter—and he was not deny-
ing, but he was disavowing his Jewishness. His son, Vic-
tor, was originally called Tischi, but Dirstein changed his
son's name when he became the Baron. So once Dirstein
got into the Vienna opera during the performance of
Parsifal, which was always performed at Easter in Vienna, and in the scene where the holy grail appears, he
shouted in full voice: *"Matzoknödel,"* matzoballs. He was,
of course, arrested immediately.

The more interesting thing is the following, this man
was five years in analysis with Freud, and when he came
to me I was quite a young analyst. Freud sent him to

me, and there was a reason for that. Dirstein had been a masochist, sexual masochist, he got his sexual relaxation or sexual orgasm when he let himself be beaten by a woman. There was the following story. He hired a woman, one of these passionate amateurs, a better type of woman, and went with her to a hotel and instructed her. First, she had to accuse him, reproach him for something, and then she had to use the word *"Du"* to him in German. Then he bent down, and she gave him a slap on the behind. Now, the story of the whole perversion came out during analysis. Since he had been five years in analysis, he could explain and interpret to me as a young analyst. He knew more than I. Five years daily with Freud, think of that.

The original scene was the following. Dirstein's father had the habit of whenever one of the women of the house, his wife, sister, maid, passed him by he gave her a great slap on the behind. And the little boy originally imitated the adult; he identified with father. Later on he shifted into the feminine, he identified with the woman. At the time he came to me, he was not anymore a masochist, he was on the contrary, a little sadistic. I bent him on the other side. And at this time, he did the following. You probably don't remember in Vienna the Kärtnerstrasse, it is comparable to Fifth Avenue here in New York. Whenever a woman passed by, he slapped her on the behind. It was evening mostly, late evening. And once—and that was the first time I went with Freud to court—Dirstein slapped the behind of a woman, and she turned around and slapped his face. And he shouted: *"Du Trampel Ich bin ja selber ein sadist"*—"You tramp, I am the sadist around here." It was a crowd on the Kärtnerstrasse in the evening. Police came, and he was taken to the police station and accused of disorderly conduct. And Freud and I went to court to testify for him that he was a patient. Freud told me I should at this time be as restrained as possible

—when they ask questions say a minimum, so that I shouldn't give anything away of the story of the patient.

Now, Dirstein wrote a little novel, in which he told, so to speak, his whole story. Quite a humorous novel, quite nice, too. He wrote, for instance, that a woman who is very well-dressed cannot be unhappy, and a woman who is unhappy cannot be well-dressed. It is quite true. He said in his book that he was in a higher milieu, he was in Vienna on a diplomatic mission. And he wrote the story with himself as a double, he meets a person who is a double of his. And Kokoshka, whose pictures now are many thousands of dollars, drew pictures for this book. I regret that I cannot show it to you because my son has it.

At this time when he came to me, he had conquered entirely his masochism and perversion, but he made mercilessly fun of himself. The whole Vienna roared with laughter at his *bon mots* and the funny things he said about himself. They were circulated as jokes.

DR. FREEMAN: Would you call the process—after he got rid of this particular perversion and then made fun of himself in his book—a kind of sublimation?

DR. REIK: I wouldn't say sublimation, because sublimation means that you use an originally sexual or aggressive activity for, so to speak, a higher social aim. That was not the case with him. It was personal.

DR. REIK: Here is a book which I recommend to you, and about which we shall talk if you read German fluently. Here, take it home. Freud sent the author an enthusiastic letter when she sent him the book. They were both refugees in London then—it was during the war. She was a very strange woman. She came to me when I was in Berlin. Her name was Rachel Berdach, and she was married at this time, and very rich; she had a sister also in Berlin. She had many neurotic symptoms. I treated her for a long time and got rid of all her symptoms, except one thing. She had this book in her mind and could not write one line of it. That means she could in analysis tell me the book word for word. It is in rhythmical prose. And she could recite the book from one end to the other, but she could not write down one line. Once she let herself be put by a friend into a room where there was ink, paper and pens, and a toilet, nothing else. And she was fourteen days in this room, and she didn't write one word. Later on she gave a lecture for the benefit of the Jewish community in Berlin when the Nazis were already there. And she stood up and could for two hours recite this book. It was like burned into her memory, but she couldn't write it.

Then the following happened. She lost all her money by the Nazis. Her husband went off with another woman, got divorced. She escaped to London and she survived the worst days of the Blitz in London. I lived at this time in the Hague in Holland. She came to Holland and then we worked that through. She finally wrote the book and it was printed in Vienna. And then the Nazis came and burned the book with so many others.

DR. FREEMAN: But when she had lost everything, she could do the book.

DR. REIK: Yes, then she could do the book. What she had was a tremendous fear of the death of someone dear to her. So you can see it was a terrible guilt feeling because such fears are also wishes. The guilt feeling was directed against her mother and sister. Well, I explained it in the Introduction to the English translation of the book, which was called *The Emperor, The Sages and Death*. And I quoted Freud there in which he said: "I like your mysteriously beautiful book so much that I can hardly judge it. It is the moving transfiguration of Jewish suffering, or the surprise in reading of it in the Court of the ingenious and tyrannical German emperor [Frederick the Second] who understood the wisdom of psychoanalysis so well, that I must say a long time has passed since I read such a meaningful and poetically successful book. After this, the hesitancy in your letter: Does your modesty prevent you from recognizing your own value? Who are you? Where did you get all the fine thoughts expressed in your book. Judging from your concern with the problem of death, it seems that you are very young."

He invited her to see him and they spent the afternoon in talking. She wrote to me that Freud was very astonished that I didn't tell him about her. But I thought I would postpone it until the book is written. I always hoped that I could present him the book, but it was too late. I had already left Holland for America, and I never saw him again.

Dr. Freeman: Would you say there is a guilt component in a writing block?

Dr. Reik: In general, I would not say that. But in this case there was. And there was something else. She was one of these women who long years before the Nazis came had this feeling of impending calamity. She always said she leads a *nécessaire* existence. "*Nécessaire*" was called in Vienna, and in Paris too, a little box or pack in which are only the most necessary things. And she said she led a *nécessaire* existence because she is always prepared that something terrible would happen to her.

Dr. Freeman: And, of course, to write the book means to become involved.

Dr. Reik: Yes, and besides that she was shying away from what she thought might be fame. I didn't hear from her very much later on, and she is an old woman now—she was older than I.

DR. FREEMAN: She never did become famous.

DR. REIK: No, she never did.

DR. FREEMAN: One doesn't have to be afraid of fame. It's the least likely thing to happen anyway.

DR. REIK: Yes, good. But she was as a woman—how would I say—very prudish, of which you will see traces in the book too.

CHILDREN

Dr. Reik: I found in my folders a paper which I wrote about what we call in German, "*Kindermund*," bright sayings of children. I tried to bring out in that paper the wisdom which children show. I give you two instances of quite nice children's sayings. A little girl is with her family at the sea, and she says: "Mama, my body takes so much water out from the sea, the sea will get quite empty." So the idea is that the sea would get exhausted with so much water out. The second which I noted there is the following. A very little peasant girl sees a painter who paints a landscape, and he is entirely engrossed in his work. She sits behind him, and suddenly she says: "I have measles." She wants to give him an interesting piece of news.

Also my little grandchild, her mother, my son's wife, is French. And this little girl is brought up bilingually— she speaks with her father English and with her mother French. So she will see a picture and she says to her father: "Man with beard." And then she looks at her mother and says: *"Homme avec barbe,"* as if her mother doesn't understand English.

But I add here something which I read in a German book. It is by two professors of psychology—David Katz and his wife—and I was asked to write a preface. They both taught psychology and their book, I concluded, is Gestalt psychology. It seems both were killed by the Nazis. In this very interesting book they tell a story. They follow the behavior pattern of their little boy to the fifth year, and there are some delightful sayings of his. For instance, the following: The little boy asks his mother whether she was sewing on buttons also when his father was a little boy. That shows his transcendence of time, no? Then he heard that his father David was in the First World War and he asked him (he had heard some Biblical stories) whether he also fought with Goliath—because the father is called David, of course. So the names and hindsense of children is interesting.

DR. FREEMAN: In other words, the child's sense of time is not exactly the same as ours.

DR. REIK: I also say in that paper that these stories give only one side of the sayings of children. And sometimes they falsify the picture of what children are like, because they give only one side.

And the comical is there because we are first feeling superior to the child. Freud said: "The comical results from an *Ausnahmsdifferenz.*" That means a difference of expenditure, intellectually and physically. The child falls down. We can walk, the child cannot walk. Or intellectually that he makes mistakes which we wouldn't make. So Freud said that is *Ausnahmsdifferenz.*

When we speak about the sayings of children, we react to another aspect which is gone from children when they become adults. I give there two instances. A British patient I once treated in Vienna remembers that he stood with his sister, who was three years older, by the window of their house in the country. He saw the cows return from the pasture and he said: "Can you imagine Uncle Harry being a cow?" Now, here is certainly another kind of comic. First because in the previous instance when we hear about the little girl who is afraid that the body will exhaust the sea, and the other little girl, who gives the stranger an interesting piece of news, we know exactly what the child means. But here, in this saying: "Can you imagine Uncle Harry being a cow?" it sounds, of course, entirely silly or nonsensical. He could have said: "What if he were an ox?" But he didn't say that; he said, "Cow." We don't understand what he says, but nevertheless what he says is full of meaning. And it is very interesting. The children have seen very often that the cows come home every evening, and they've seen that the cows sometimes playfully jump at each other. A few weeks before, it occurred that Aunt Muriel, the wife of Uncle Harry will have a baby. And the little boy knows about sexual intercourse and what the male does is jump on the woman like the cows did. And now the question: "Can you imagine Uncle Harry being a cow?" makes full sense. It means can you imagine that Uncle Harry did that to Aunt Muriel so that she got pregnant. It has, so to speak, to be translated into children's language.

There is another childhood memory in the same case. He asked his sister whether the telegraph post and the lamppost can speak to each other. That had its reason in the fact that he heard the droning noises the telegraph post made. We approach here the Never-Never land of Peter Pan. And a kind of area in which the child follows his own idea.

Also in the analysis of a grownup woman there was a childhood memory. As a child she sneaked in the night from her bedroom to the sitting room to find out how the furniture would behave when no one is in the room. She thought it behaved differently.

DR. FREEMAN: Isn't this an illustration of the tendency children have to anthropomorphism?

DR. REIK: Yes. I believe we should collect such sayings from the childhood memories of patients and others, to find out a new source of information about the psychology of children at different ages.

From Dr. Reik's Personal Notes

MAN

Dreams of glory are either delusions or anticipations of urgently wished future possibilities. In both cases, they are deceptive. They lead invariably to resignation and to a feeling of futility—even in the rare case that those juvenile daydreams are actually realized. Glory is only in the future or in the past; it has no experiential present.

Man is not made to progress or even regress without a promise of reward or of pleasure. Like the tortoise, man will not move unless you dangle some meal in front of his nose.

Not only liars believe finally in the stories they made up themselves, also writers do. Gustave Flaubert felt in his own mouth the taste of poison that his Madame Bovary took.

In order to become famous, a man has to come up to expectations, first to his own, then to those of all persons around him. Finally a legend will form itself about him and he is expected to live up to this legend.

We all see during our lifetime that what we considered an impossibility for ourselves twenty or even ten years ago has become a reality and we do not even wonder about it any longer.

Although Hamlet emphasized the significance of brevity for the quality of wit, our psychological exploration still pays too little attention to the importance of this factor. Here is an instance of a witty remark which shows that trait. Marshall Goering told a British diplomat that he planned to go to Poland hunting. The British diplomat remarked: "Animals, I presume."

I am dissatisfied with the teaching of history as it is done in our schools and colleges. History is not only the study of the past but of the past from which the present emerges and which is continued in our day. We speak, for instance, of the human sacrifices which the ancient peoples—the Aztecs, the Philistines, and many other nations of antiquity—almost all made to their gods. We are astonished by the barbaric customs, the cruelty and the bloodthirstiness of those people. And we? Don't we sacrifice millions of men, women and children to a national or social ideal? How about the crematoria, the gas chambers, and so on. The only difference is that those nations of antiquity sacrificed people to their god and we sacrifice men to an idea, which is nothing but the god of our time. Compared with the cruelty which emerges in those sacrifices of our time, the deeds of savage nations were benevolent charitableness.

The two activities considered the most secret and private

ones, namely excretion and sexual intercourse, are biologically as well as genetically connected. There is no doubt that excretion is, in evolutionary terms, the older form, from which the conjugation of the protozoa developed.

It is remarkable that no food was made a god or goddess to be worshipped together with that food. Remnants in the ancient religions (Bacchus, Ceres in ancient Rome, for instance) indicate that there were cults of that character in prehistoric times. It is as if a faint echo of such worship reaches us when we read that Heinrich Heine said of a certain dish: "One should eat it only kneeling down."

A great Marrano poet wrote an elegy on three Marrano martyrs in 1665 and gave it the title *"Contra la verdad no hay fuerza"* (Against truth, force does not avail). This adage could serve as the device against all persecution of displeasing scientific insights.

It sometimes occurs to us that our pity for others is superfluous. It never occurs to us that our self-pity is superfluous.

MEN AND WOMEN

There is only one race for men that's more passionate than running after money. This other race is running after sexual satisfaction.

When a man is in a romantic mood, he thinks, "this girl." When he is at some melancholic weekend mood, he imagines, "some girl." When he is sexually excited, "any girl."

The beauty cult of women threatens to push aside every other religion. Whereas our grandmothers tried to make peace with the Creator, our women try their "make-up." Being a woman requires hard work. It is not enough to be created as a woman, every beauty salon knows that. One has to be made a woman!

A little story circulating in New York at present may very well be transferred from the oral to the sexual area: An old bachelor finally married a much younger woman. Asked by a friend why he got married, the man answered: "I could not stand to eat in various restaurants any longer." After half a year the same friend runs into the man again and asks him: "How do you like home cooking?" The man answers: "Now I like again to eat at various restaurants."

Women try to understand men and succeed without making a great effort. Men make a great effort to understand women, but they never succeed.

"In the beginning was rhythm" said the composer Hans von Bulow. That is true not only in music but also in lovemaking. It is the timing that determines if the performance is a success or a failure.

A single girl who cannot stay away even for a few hours from her home: Analysis shows that the girl is afraid that her mother, who is healthy and vigorous, would die in her absence. Behind this fear is, of course, the unconscious wish for her mother's death.

You often hear that a man has got tired of a woman and left her. Why is it that woman rarely gets tired of a man and leaves him?

If men were completely sincere they would tell you that their fantasies with regard to women have nothing to do with romance and love, but with sex. And this means sex in the raw. Rarely with prostitutes or whores but with the memory of a certain woman in whom the female is, so to speak, personified. The fantasy of the man can be focused on certain movements or positions of that woman, for instance how she spread her legs apart or had her legs high in the air during sexual intercourse. It has nothing to do with the personality of this woman, whom he could even despise. His fantasy is about her lovemaking.

A psychologist in one of my seminars stated his theory about some essential psychological differences between the sexes. He asserted that only men expect some miraculous experience from sexuality, as if they hoped to find again a kind of bliss once felt. Women do not expect this from sexuality but from love. He traced those differences back to childhood: the boy wants to re-experience the first sexual arousal, while the girl hopes to find again the happiness she experienced as a child in being loved by mother. I could not help but remark in the ensuing discussion: "Both expectations will be frustrated."

A second psychiatrist turned our attention to another factor which he made responsible for those psychological differences. He pointed out that the expectancy of newness in the male is considerably determined by the secret location of the female genitals and is to a great extent based on the sexual curiosity of the little boy, a curiosity whose existence is continued in the adult. In little girls that initial sexual curiosity is easily satisfied and is almost nonexistent in the grownup woman, whose question in this direction is perhaps transferred to the problem: "How will he make love to me?"

The old adage that he who is unlucky in cards is lucky in love, has a good psychological meaning. If a young man is unlucky in his card-playing, he perhaps is thinking of a woman and does not pay proper attention to his cards. Love is exclusive, and like the God of the Old Testament, does not tolerate another god beside it.

"If wishes were beggars . . ." If desires were actions, promiscuity would be the general and unexceptional rule on earth.

The jealousy of men is mostly visual. They call up hateful images of sexual intercourse their wives or mistresses have with lovers. Women, however often they suffer from jealousy, are not often tormented by those terrible pictures that are hell for men.

The enjoyment of sexual intercourse is also determined by its emotional consequence, which is either an afterglow or an aftermath.

It is interesting to imagine the behavior and the emotions of the two sexes in the same situation. Take the case of a woman who thinks of her looks, this very thought can cheer her up or make her depressed. Can the same thought lead to identical emotional consequences in a man?

They say that a word is dead when it is said. That is true for men, who say loving things or give compliments to a woman. But it is not true for that woman. For her that word is only asleep and when she is alone she awakens it to new life and fondles it.

There is a certain type of woman who tries to take a man away from another woman—even from her friend— though she does not really want the man for herself. It is as if such women want only to reassure themselves that they are sexually more attractive than the other woman. Such competition, whereby the object itself is almost a matter of indifference, is very rare between men. That means very few men will try to get the wife, mistress, or bride of any other man if they do not care for her or if they do not desire the woman for herself.

A man is in the worst emotional attitude toward a woman when he is afraid of her.

Women are closer to the original conscience than men; that means they regress to the phase in which conscience reflected what others, the parents and other people, said about them when they were little girls. Public opinion that later takes the place of those representative figures has a greater influence upon women than upon men. The voice of conscience for woman often has the form: "There will be talk."

Preverbal communication: Here is a little everyday observation. I stood beside two college girls who, as myself, waited before the public library until it opened at nine A.M. One girl looked away to the clock on the other side to see how late or rather how early it was. In this moment a young man appeared with books in his hands. The one girl looked at her friend, who must have felt the glance, because she turned around. And now the first girl turned the attention of her friend to the young man who had just arrived. How did she turn her friend's attention to him? In glancing at her girlfriend and then glancing at the young man. It was as if she had said: "Here he is, the young fellow about whom we had talked." Yet not a single word was said by either of the two girls. They communicated only on glances. Men do such things very rarely. I would not go so far as to assert that it is impossible for them; it is just not done. Such preverbal communication in the case of men can be compared to a road that is present, but is rarely used.

When my sister serves me a cup of coffee, she stirs the

coffee with the spoon—as if she would not trust me to do that myself. Women's care goes sometimes too far.

Marguerite de Valois (1553-1615) said: "In love, as in war, a fortress that parleys is half taken."

It is easy for a woman to observe a young man without his being aware of it. It is almost impossible for this young man to observe a young woman without her becoming aware of it.

When a woman says: "I am going to change," meaning that she will change her dress, it is significant. A woman who changes her clothes is indeed a new woman.

Women are more realistic than men even when they are romantically involved. They can clearly see the weaknesses and shortcomings of their men and still love them. Their love needs not to be blind.

What does sexual intercourse essentially amount to? Repeated friction at the right place.

A woman who does not feel sexually aroused at all nonetheless wishes to be sexually desirable, and desired by the man, and feels hurt if she is not.

Sexual fantasies that are imagined for a long period, by and by lose their arousing effect. They are subjected to the law of diminishing returns.

A slip: One young woman who glided into a sexual relationship with a married man said that he was not in a position to take care of her needs at that point. She had to pretend to be independent, which she didn't really feel. "He also started a casual relationship with another girl who he impregnated and this was a painful blow, even though I don't consider it a deep betrayal. In fact it was partly an attempt to put a brake on his increasing involvement with me, which is too much for him. His wife troubles him greatly and is in a disturbed state, and he is determined to stick by her until she gets help." These passages are taken from a letter of the young woman to her psychoanalyst during the summer vacation. The first sentence here quoted contains an orthographic or grammatical slip which is conspicuous since she is college educated. The slip is the following, "He also started a casual relationship with a girl who he impregnated." Here the first case appears instead of the accusative "whom he impregnated." The psychoanalytic exploration of this slip will depart from an attentive analysis of the sentence following the slip, but first we have to remark that the writer speaks of a "casual" relationship of that man as if she wanted to minimize the meaning of it. Yet it was a painful blow, although "not a deep betrayal." She still tries to find extenuating circumstances and exonerating reasons for the loved man: "His increasing involvement with me is too much," "his wife troubles him greatly." Considering these circumstances, the conclusion is justified that the slip is unconsciously determined by the letter-writer's thought that not the man, but the other girl with whom he had an affair wanted to get pregnant. The slip "with another girl who he impregnated" attributes an active part to the woman, at least in the writer's wishful thinking.

Man shows at all times that he is a beast, but especially in the morning before he has his breakfast coffee.

A mother thinking of her baby: "A poor thing, but my own."

Some men listening to women sometimes think that one

needs the patience of a saint to stand the chatter, without imagining that the real saints are the women who bear with men.

She gets slim. Is it diet or is it love?

Some pharmacies sell pills which make you fall quickly asleep, but which don't prevent you from awakening after a short time and spending a sleepless night in which you toss and turn in your bed, try to read and so on. Love is to be compared to those deceptive and abortive sleeping pills. When you fall in love, you believe it is forever. After a short time you awaken and recognize that you are sober and you have remained alone.

Women who put their husbands on display before other women still remain feminine. A man who wants to show off his new mistress before other men has decidedly strong feminine trends.

One of the essential preconditions for romantic feelings of a man is sexual frustration. The proof for this is that romance dies, whether slowly or suddenly, after sexual satisfaction with its object.

When a woman says to a man: "You're the boss," she knows that he is in bondage to her.

The American colloquialism for sexual intercourse is "having fun." As a matter of fact, it is now taken very seriously and it is not funny any longer.

Men often wonder how "childish" women are. But in general they are not children at all, and are more mature than men. They are only childlike in many regards. If they were not childlike, how could they take such wonderful care of children? More than this, how could they even understand children?

A woman preparing a party may think: "The people come to see me and not my apartment," but while she puts her apartment in order and beautifies it, she acts as if she and her apartment were a single unit—another confirmation of the validity of the psychoanalytic theory that conceives of a room as of an unconscious symbol for a woman's body.

A woman without a man is a woman without a body; a man without a woman is a man with only a body.

There is no doubt that women in general are less cruel physically than men. The problem not yet solved is whether this is due to biological or to psychological factors, that is, to constitutional or educational differences.

A woman who feels that a man is frightened of her is filled with contempt for him.

The majority of women would tolerate rather the brutalities of a man than his weakness.

Gallantry: many American girls in their twenties are not yet accustomed to men's gallant manners. The other day I flew from New York to Atlanta and the pretty stewardess who led me to my seat at the airplane, said: "Please follow me." I said: "With pleasure." And, by God, she deeply blushed. No European girl who had outgrown her puberty years would blush at such a remark. She would take it for granted.

Very few things said at parties sound as malicious and as insincere as they are.

Women cannot be convinced by words. In the best case they can be *persuaded* by talking. Only a kiss is convincing.

✿

WHAT PATIENTS SAY

A middle aged man: "It is not true what the statisticians assert, that married men live longer than bachelors. Married life becomes so boring that it only appears to the husbands much longer."

A middle aged man: "I just drove on a bus past the apartment I had five years ago. I remembered the wonderful time I had there when Jane came to visit me. We often did not get up from the bed the whole day. Yet if I would meet her again it would not be the same any longer. I have changed and I am sure that she has. Who knows how many lovers she has had in the meantime. No, it would not be the same anymore. The memories I have kept are certainly more beautiful than the reality was."

Young woman in first interview: "I was married to him for one year. What sex with him was like, you ask? The less said about it the better—and there is damned little to say about it." The same woman about another man, two years of promiscuous life later: "He was the greatest . . . I never experienced anything like it."

Another woman: "When all is done in bed, not all is said—you understand, don't you?"

A young man about a girl: "She sat down across from me in such a way that a considerable part of her underwear was visible. I didn't know whether she was flirtatious or only careless."

A middle aged man: "I found that the need to smoke is at least as urgent and imperative as the sexual drive."

An Irishwoman, middle aged: "You know, I have that fighting spirit from my parents and from their parents.

We Irish all have it. My father once told me a story: An Irishman walked on the street late in the evening and happened to see two groups of men in a violent scuffle. He asked: 'Is this a private fight or is it a free-for-all in which I can participate too?' "

Young girl: "He kissed me and I him. In the middle of our kissing I was worried whether my hem is uneven."

Young man about a woman: "I was very shy with her in the beginning until I told myself that she too has to go to the bathroom several times during the day."

Another man about his sexual life: "You know, my wife gave me *carte blanche*. What more can a philandering husband wish? But I need that guiltiness, those furtive and secret relations."

A woman who is a secretary: "My previous boss was straightforward and when he did not like something, he said so. The present is very considerate, but often he becomes devious in order not to hurt people's feelings and we sense that, of course, and sometimes feel much more hurt than otherwise."

A man about his relationship with his wife: "I realize only now that underneath any extreme consideration for her is an unyielding will of my own."

A woman about her husband: "When we are at parties, he makes suggestive remarks to other women and almost propositions them in my presence. I wish he would already sleep with one of them. I would prefer that to this behavior. He does not see that it humiliates me and hurts my feelings . . ." Ten minutes later: "We have two beds and I knew, of course, that he wanted me to come into his bed, but I have my pride too. He should come to me."

Another woman: "When we are in company, he sits with his arm around me and takes my hand. I am tired out because he never shows me affection when we are alone. Not even in sexual intercourse does he show that he cares for me. I expect at least a pat or another affectionate move from him the next morning but there is nothing. It is as if nothing happened between us a few hours ago!"

A man about the others in his office: "The Jews among them are warm and sometimes even helpful. They are all so unsuspicious."

A man about his wife: "I bought some nude pictures of women when I went on Forty-second Street. At home I looked at them, but I expected that Jane could come into the room any moment. My feeling was exactly that of a little boy who masturbates and is afraid that mother would catch him." A few minutes later: "I hate her because she makes me feel guilty."

Another man about his wife: "I know she is surprised with my success and my career. I sometimes wish to be failure, because I want her to love me as I am—even if I fail. Yes, then even more than otherwise."

Time heals all wounds, except the hidden ones.

In many cases, psychoanalysis has the result that the patient after it or during its last months would be able to become a good wife or husband, an appropriate spouse. "But," the patients ask, "where are the suitable partners?" and seem to expect that psychoanalysts also direct a marriage bureau.

Dream of a patient: He sees a big rat sitting behind him that looks at him with small penetrating eyes. Interpretation: the "rat" is the psychoanalyst.

Theodor Reik died on December 31, 1969.

INDEX

abortion, 62, 68
Abraham, Karl, 2, 89, 92, 94, 110-111, 117
Adler, Alfred, 1, 95, 108-109, 113
adultery, 71, 189
aggression, direction of, 22-23
agoraphobia, 95
ambition, 15
American analysts, 107
anality, 164, 207
anatomy, 121, 140
anthropomorphism, 220
anti-Semitism, 158-162
anxiety, 14, 27
appearances, concern with, 131, 135, 147-148, 224
Arnold, Matthew, 129
arousal process, sexual, 144
Astor, Lady, 126

Balzac, Honoré de, 25
basic rules in analysis, 19, 27
Beer-Hoffman, 90, 188
Beethoven, Ludwig van, 54, 99
Berdach, Rachel, 213-216
Bergler, Edmund, 103
belle dame sans merci, La, 145

bigotry, 158
Bonaparte, Princess Marie, 82-83, 86, 91, 118
Brahms, Johannes, 99
Brill, A. A., 95
Bruckner, Anton, 205
Bülow, Hans von, 224
Burlingham, Dorothy, 92-93
Bychowski, Gustav, 4

castration fear, 139, 146
castration wish, 65
Chansons de ma vie, Les (Guilbert), 170
Chaplin, Charlie, 89, 170-171
character armor, 110
characteristic trait, normal, 15
Chateaubriand, François René de, 25
childbirth, 149
childhood, pathology of, 40
children:
    analysis for, 17, 81-82
    early guilt feelings in, 38-40
    need for love in, 31-32, 114, 158
    sayings of, interpreted, 217-220